GRACE (EVENTUALLY)

GRACE (EVENTUALLY)

THOUGHTS ON FAITH

ANNE LAMOTT

LARGE PRINT PRESS

A part of Gale, Cengage Learning

GALE
CENGAGE Learning

Detroit • New York • San Francisco • New Haven, Conn • Waterville, Maine • London

GALE
CENGAGE Learning™

Copyright © 2007 by Anne Lamott.
Pages 283–284 constitutes an extension of this copyright page.
Large Print Press, a part of Gale, Cengage Learning.

The text of this Large Print edition is unabridged.
Other aspects of the book may vary from the original edition.
Set in 16 pt. Plantin.
Printed on permanent paper.

LIBRARY OF CONGRESS CATALOGING-IN-PUBLICATION DATA

Lamott, Anne.
    Grace(eventually) : thoughts on faith / by Anne Lamott.
      p. cm.
    Originally published: New York : Riverhead Books, 2007.
    ISBN-13: 978-0-7862-9622-4 (hardcover : alk. paper)
    ISBN-10: 0-7862-9622-4 (hardcover : alk. paper)
      1. Lamott, Anne — Religion. 2. Novelists, American — 20th century — Biography. 3. Christian biography — United States. 4. Faith. 5. Large type books. I. Title.
    PS3562.A4645Z464 2007b
    813'.54—dc22
                                                        [B] 2007010240

ISBN 13: 978-1-59413-265-0 (pbk. : alk. paper)
ISBN 10: 1-59413-265-8 (pbk. : alk. paper)
Published in 2008 by arrangement with Riverhead Books, a member of Penguin Group (USA) Inc.

Printed in the United States of America
1 2 3 4 5 6 7 12 11 10 09 08

For Sam

And for the kids and youth
of St. Andrew,
who taught me how to be a teacher

And for the kids and youth
of Marin City

Love you, bless you, keep you.

CONTENTS

7

Where is the Life we have lost in living?
— T. S. Eliot

PRELUDE

There is not much truth being told in the world. There never was. This has proven to be a major disappointment to some of us. When I was a child, I thought grown-ups and teachers knew the truth, because they told me they did. It took years for me to discover that the first step in finding out the truth is to begin unlearning almost everything adults had taught me, and to start doing all the things they'd told me *not* to do. Their main pitch was that achievement equaled happiness, when all you had to do was study rock stars, or movie stars, or them, to see that they were mostly miserable. They were all running around in mazes like everyone else.

On the other hand, sometimes you encountered people who'd stopped playing everyone else's game, who seemed to be semi-happy, and *with* it, who said, in so many words, I saw the cheese, I lived on it for years, and it wasn't worth it. It was plain old Safeway Swiss.

At twenty-one, I still believed that if you could only get to see sunrise at Stonehenge, or full moon at the Taj Mahal, you would be nabbed by truth. And then you would be well, and able to relax and feel fully alive. But I actually knew a few true things: I had figured out that truth and freedom were pretty much the same. And that almost everyone was struggling to wake up, to be loved, and not feel so afraid all the time. That's what the cars, degrees, booze, and drugs were about.

By the time I had dropped out of college at nineteen, I'd acquired a basic and wildly ecumenical faith cobbled together from shards I'd gathered in reading various wisdom traditions — Native American, Hindu, feminist, Buddhist, even Christian, in a heart-stopping, kick-starting encounter with Kierkegaard's *Fear and Trembling*. My best teachers were mess, failure, death, mistakes, and the people I hated, including myself.

Drugs often helped. I knew that if you had the eyes to see, there was beauty everywhere, even when nature was barren or sloppy, and not just when God had tarted things up for the spring. Often the people with the deepest insight looked as ordinary as any old alcoholic or serial killer. They *might* look like Siddhartha or Ananda Mai Ma, but odds were they resembled your bipolar cousin Ruth, or Mr. Burns from *The Simpsons*. Also, they could be extremely annoying. I already understood that on this side of eternity, we were not going to get over much or see very clearly, and that often what we saw was happening only in our minds: "Things are not as they seem. Nor are they otherwise." Who said this? Rumi? Or Illya Kuryakin? No idea.

Thirty years ago, I was living in Bolinas, California, an exquisite enclave of hippies, artists, and organic farmers on the coast. I had a wonderful poet boyfriend named Ty. We were crazy about each other, even though we were not exclusive — which is to say that I loved him more than he loved me. But he was gentle and funny, and had great stories about his years in India, Tibet, Taos, and Salt Lake City. It had never occurred to me before Ty that you might wake up spiritually as easily in Utah as in Sri Lanka. He was the first to give me books from which I learned that God was an equal opportunity employer — that it was possible to experience the divine anywhere you were, anywhere you could see the sun and moon rise or set, or burn through the fog.

Bolinas was a great place for ritual and celebrations — it was nearly as exotic as India, if you thought about it, but without all those dying animals in the streets and people defecating in the holy waters, which doesn't really work for me at all. We had perfectly good bodily mess right here where I lived. We had burnouts in the streets, nudes on the beach, our own drunken sex lives. Feral cats, three-legged dogs, and horses stood side by side. During our countless festivals and parades, people in cowboy boots and homemade holiday garlands and leis drank beer, and vivid chalk murals decorated the walls downtown — an exuberant aesthetic that celebrated both ordinary community life and tribal-stomp mysticism, but on the Pacific Coast instead of the Ganges. There were altars and candles and veils, people in costume and exotic clothing redolent of human spirit and dreams — not to mention foods cooking in the heat, all that delicious joy, with rot waiting in the wings.

And then Ty fell head over heels in love with another woman, who had so many unfair advantages over me. For instance, she was not a falling-down drunk. She was womanly and celestial. She had money and perfect earth-mother clothes of flowing silk, batiked and embroidered, and soft blond hair, whereas I was poor and looked like a Gypsy wagon with fuzzy curls. She was a gifted artist, soft-spoken and gentle, with an elegant house on the beach, all candles, altars, incense. She even had a beautiful name: Romy.

She did not love Ty as much as he loved her, or as much as I loved him, which stacked the deck in her favor. In the competition between us, she won for caring less. After Ty and I had been sleeping together for six months or so, he left me for her.

I had already come through three heartbreaks, which caused long physical withdrawals, as bad as trying to get off cigarettes, and through two bad acid trips, and everyone convinced me that I would come through this bad patch, too. Luckily I was still drinking. And I had a perfect best friend, whom I saw every day and who drank the way I did.

I learned mostly from drugs and great books: I was a lifelong reading girl.

I already believed that there was something in me that could not be touched or destroyed that you could call the soul. And I was part of two wings of the community — the smartest, funniest alcoholics, and the seekers, who had designed lives based on spiritual values and tried to live up to them. I loved equally reading the great literature of the world and getting wasted. I thought we were here to have spiritual awakenings. When it came to books or drugs, I'd take anything that was offered, and I considered the next day's drug hangover worth the expanded sense of reality. I was sick many mornings, but curious, like Dorothy opening her eyes in Oz: Is there still gravity? Can we breathe the air? Yes. Then might as well go look around.

I was crushed for a while after Ty dumped me, but it really *is* easier to experience spiritual connection when your life is in the process of coming apart. When things break up and fences fall over, desperation and powerlessness slink in, which turns out to be good: humility and sweetness often arrive in your garden not long after. And I had a pharmacist friend in San Francisco who gave me Valium. The tears were finally helpful, for what they washed away and revealed, which is to say my deep longing for a kind partner, and my bad judgment. Seeds sank into the ground, and who could even guess what might grow? Hey! We all like surprises, don't we?

My best friend and my father and younger

brother saw me through; they helped keep the patient as comfortable as could be expected. I finally figured out that I had a choice: I could suffer a great deal, or not, or for a long time. Or I could have the combo platter: suffer, breathe, pray, play, cry, and try to help people. There was meaning in pain; it taught you how to survive with a modicum of grace when you did not get what you wanted. In addition, I got a couple of office-temp boyfriends, and best of all, lost a lot of weight.

By June 1975, life had gotten easier. We were in the delicious bland limbo of Gerald Ford. Our generation had changed the world: the worst U.S. president in history had been forced to resign, the war in Vietnam had at last ended, and the women's movement was here to stay. On one particular day, I was bird-watching at the Bolinas lagoon with my father, and at a certain hour he left to make my younger brother dinner down the road. Not long after he left, Ty stepped through the willows and alders onto the bank where I sat.

We hugged and kissed, and I buried myself in his smells. We smoked a joint and huddled in the chill of dusk. He gave me his sweater. We marveled at the ducks and egrets on the calm waters, white pelicans flying overhead.

He told me that Romy and he were still together, but she wanted to sleep with other men. Although he loved her, he spent only a couple of nights a week at her house. I thought this over. "Oh," I said. "Which nights?" He laughed.

He was so handsome, sweet, and so much fun. He asked if I wanted to come to his house for enchiladas. Of course I did. We ate them with a lot of hot sauce and cold Tecate, and went to bed. We could not get enough of each other. Eventually he fell asleep, and I turned on the reading light. The book beside his bed was *The Only Dance There Is,* which was based in part on lectures on spirituality that Ram Dass had given at the Menninger Foundation. A few people had told me how brilliant and funny it was, and I dove in with cheerful anticipation.

I got to the title page, where there was a calligraphed inscription from Romy, with curlicue hearts, lotuses, and — I am not making this up — a drawing of Krishna.

Hmph, I thought, and put it aside. I found *Trout Fishing in America* and reread parts. In the morning when I awoke, Ty was at the foot of his bed, in cutoff blue jeans, tying his running shoes. "Where are you going?" I asked.

He said he was going for a long run on the ridge. But then? He paused. It was a bad pause. He was going to an outdoor luncheon at Romy's. I tried to act nonchalant, and did not start crying until he left. Then I lay on my side, naked, and sobbed for so long that I was heaving for breath, for every man who hadn't loved me enough. I showered, brushed my teeth, took some aspirin, found some Visine in his medicine chest, dressed in my tie-dyed tank top and underpants, and crawled back into bed. When Ty returned, he was clearly worried to see me still there. I said I had been throwing up and had a fever.

He looked as if he might be about to burp up a newborn chick.

He got me a cup of tea with honey, toast with honey, yogurt with honey, like I was John the Baptist with the flu. He said he had to take a shower and then head over to Romy's. I said it was totally okay, but I was just too sick to get up. He felt my forehead with the back of his hand, like a father. I was hot from crying and grief and mental illness. He went to shower.

When he came back, I clutched my stomach as if I was about to heave, and he got me a pot to vomit in. This is my kind of date. I lay back in bed, barely able to keep my eyes open.

I pretended to sleep while he got dressed.

"Annie?" he said gently. I opened my eyes, waiting for the boot. "You can stay here as long as you need. But I won't be back until tomorrow."

"Okay," I said in a tiny voice. I tried to look as sick as I could, in the most touching possible way, like the little match girl in tie-dye. He made me more tea and sat with me. I cried when I heard his car drive off, but I knew he would be back later in the day. How could you leave skinny, touching, sick, adorable me? I'll show *you,* I thought: I won't leave.

Then, because I didn't know what else to do, I started to read the book Romy had given him. This was part masochism, part revenge, and part curiosity. And I was soon mesmerized. There was nothing particularly new about consciousness and God and love in the book, but it was the first time I'd heard this information given in such a hilarious, wise, human, neurotic voice. Ram Dass was a vulnerable mess — just like me. I felt the way I had felt reading *A Wrinkle in Time* at eight, *The Catcher in the Rye, Catch-22,* Virginia Woolf, Vonnegut later on, whenever a book had offered me a box with treasure inside. It was what flooded out in the quiet, intimate relationship between me and the writer; the treasure of me.

The physical excitement in me was profound. People say about experiences like this that "the veil lifted," but for me, for the whole day, it was as if an itchy burlap sack had come off my head. Molecules shifted, as in the shimmer before a migraine, the ocular shift at the edges, where I felt as if I might be having a stroke. Ram Dass's book was about his stuckness, his sick ego, his life, his heart, the Buddha, Krishna, his guru — even Jesus, which was truly radical. I felt as though I were snorkeling one concentric circle outside where I had been before.

I read all afternoon in bed, peaceful as a cat. There was only me, the book, the space I was reading in; hands, and the whisper of pages, eyes, and a place to sprawl. The wrinkly flower of my heart was opening in slow motion. I felt one with everybody. Well, except Romy. I felt about one and a half with her, even as I knew deep inside that she was part of the reason that I would never be the same. And I wasn't.

This was the day I pecked a hole out of the cocoon and saw the sky of ingredients that would constitute my spiritual path. This was the day I knew the ingredients of the spiritual that would serve me — love, poetry, prayer, meditation, community. I knew that sex could be as sacred as taking care of the poor. I knew that no one comes holier than anyone else, that nowhere is better than anywhere else. I knew that the resurrection of the mind was possible. I knew that no matter how absurd and ironic it was, acknowledging death and the finite was what gave you life and presence. You might as well make it good. Nature, family, children, cadavers, birth, rivers in which we pee and bathe, splash and flirt and float memorial candles — in these you would find holiness.

I started praying, not the usual old prayer of "God, I am such a loser," but new ones — "Hi" and "Thank you." I viscerally got that God was everywhere; poor old God, just waiting for you to notice, and enter your life like a track coach for slow people. Kathleen Norris said, many years later, "Prayer is not asking for what you think you want, but asking to be changed in ways you can't imagine," and I got the message that day. People were going to come into my life. Many of them would leave. Most of the people in my family would roll their eyes and hope that soon I'd go back to the manic and tranquilizing mall of American life.

Ty still hadn't come back by the time I

finished reading the book at seven, so I went to the main road in Bolinas to hitchhike home. I ended up at the bar. It would be ten more years before I stopped drinking, twenty years ago today. But I remember standing there at dusk with my thumb out, euphoric and exhausted as if I'd been at the beach all day, then taken a long, hot shower to wash off all the sand.

■ ■ ■ ■

Dance Class

■ ■ ■ ■

See how the fearful chandelier
Trembles above you
Each time you open your mouth
To sing. Sing.

    — Donald Justice

SKI PATROL

Not too long ago, I was skiing in the mountains where my son, Sam, and I spend a weekend most winters. Nowadays, he instantly disappears with the hordes of snowboarders. I believe he is somewhat embarrassed to be seen with me: once, standing next to him and his friend at the bottom of a hill, I fell over for no reason. And in fact, the very first time we went skiing together, I skied in a strangely slow, inexorable path for a hundred feet or so, straight into a huge net at the bottom of the slopes, erected to protect the small Ski Bear children from being crushed. Then I got tangled up in it, like a fish.

After Sam disappears, I usually take the chairlift to the top of the pony slope for a couple of runs, which anyone can manage. And I triumph. I roar down the slight incline, pretending to be an Olympic skier. Filled with confidence, I try the easiest intermediate slope, where I mostly fall or slide down on my butt for the first run, and then have a few extended runs of four or five minutes where I am actually skiing. By my second run down an intermediate slope, I am on my feet almost the whole time, skiing triumphantly for America.

But this time, as the chairlift carried me to the top of the intermediate slope, which I had just skied down, I experienced a moment's confusion, born of hormones, high altitude, and a light snow falling. I suddenly could not remember whether the stop we were approaching was the same one I had just skied down from. The chair slowed and lowered for us to disembark, and my seatmate got off and zipped away like a swallow, while I sat there torn between wanting to get off and thinking that mine was the next stop.

The chair jerked forward and resumed its ascent. I looked around for landmarks but saw only brightly colored skiers in clusters, and I was pretty sure that this was not the right stop . . . until a second later, when I realized I was mistaken — it *was* the right stop. By then, the chair was four or five feet off the ground and rising. But I did not let this stop me. I took a long, deep breath, wriggled to the edge of the chair, and flung myself off into the snow — flung myself, the way stuntmen fling themselves onto the backs of speeding trains, or a clown flings himself from a bucking bronco, mugging bug-eyed for the crowd.

I estimate that I was five or six feet off the ground for the timeless instant of eternity before I crashed down into the snow. I landed hard, proving the theory of gravity once and for all. I was somehow still on my skis, for a moment, until I fell over.

I do not imagine anyone had seen anything like this before, someone hurtling into outer space with such force, from such a low starting point. I felt like Icarus, near death in the snow, with melting skis instead of wings.

I was immediately aware of two things: that I was not badly hurt, and that most people were pretending not to have noticed, out of kindness, or horror, or mortification. I am ever my mother's daughter, and so my first impulse was to smile with confidence to the few who were watching, wave like a politician campaigning from a rarely used horizontal position.

"I'm okay," I said to two pretty women who came over and offered to pull me up. I continued to wave nonchalantly, as if this sort of silly thing happened to me all the time. I told them that I just needed to catch my breath. They made sympathetic cooing sounds, and skied away. I sat up and leaned back on my hands in the snow.

By the time I finally stood up, my hands were frozen. I was winded, ashamed, confused, bruised — grateful only that Sam hadn't seen me. He'd have died. He would have stabbed himself repeatedly in the head with his ski pole.

Just when I thought things couldn't get much worse, nausea struck, wave after wave, like morning sickness, and I thought, I'm going to throw up in the snow! Ladies and gentlemen, now for my next trick . . . I pretended to pinch my nostrils against the cold, but was actually pressing my hand to my mouth to hold back the tide. My head spun, and I prayed, Help me, Jesus, help me, the way a very old woman at my church named Mary used to pray at her most afraid and delirious, right in the middle of anything — sermons, songs: "I know my change is gonna come, but touch me *now*, Lord."

I don't know how long I stood there with my hand clamped to my mouth, only my poles and a frayed, consignment-store faith to support me. All I knew was that help is always on the way, a hundred percent of the time. Rumi said, "Someone fills the cup in front of us." I know that when I call out,

God will be near, and hear, and help eventually. Of course, it is the "eventually" that throws one into despair. For instance, even now, I know America will be restored again, eventually, although it is hard to envision this at the moment, and it could take a century or more for the nation and the world to recover from the George W. Bush years. But they will. God always hears our cries, and helps, and it's always a surprise to see what form God will take on earth: in the old joke, a man whose plane crashed in the tundra bitterly tells a bartender that God forsook him — that he waited in vain for divine intervention, and would have died in the snow . . . if it hadn't been for some fucking *Eskimos* who came by. So maybe a tall, strong man with a medical toboggan would be by soon, or the two pretty women, or Jesus in earmuffs.

Instead, a short, plump woman pulled up on skis a few minutes later. She was wearing an orange cap and an official jacket from the ski resort.

"I think I'm going to throw up," I said, so she wouldn't get too close.

"Well, then, let's just stand here a moment," she said. She had acne and chapped cheeks, and small brown eyes.

"I think I might need help," I said, which

31

is something I force myself to say every few years.

"You landed *so* hard. I saw you from up above."

I shook my head, bewildered, on the verge of tears. "Are you on the ski patrol?" I asked.

"Sort of. I'm here to help in non-emergency situations like this. Why don't you come with me." She stepped out of her skis and stood on my bindings so that I could step out of mine. We picked up our skis and I trudged after her through the snow.

We walked to a wooden ten-by-ten shack away from the lift and went inside. It held two long benches, a folding chair, and shelves laden with first-aid equipment, bottles of water, used coffee cups, a walkie-talkie; and it was warm from a kerosene heater. There were two shabby windows, through which you could see snowy pine trees outside. The woman poured me a miniature Dixie cup of water, but my face was so cold that I couldn't get my lips to work, and I dribbled water down my front like an aged, numbed-up woman at the dentist's.

She took the cup away from me. "Let's take off your gloves first," she said, and pulled them off, as gently as if they were mittens connected inside my jacket sleeves with a string.

She laid my gloves on the chair near the heater and pulled off her own. "Mine are nice and toasty," she said. "You can wear them for a while, until yours warm up. I'll be back soon — there are only a couple of us working this spot today." She went outside.

After a while, I stretched out on one of the benches and closed my eyes. The kerosene smelled like lacquer, and I kept feeling waves of nausea. My bones were cold. I could isolate the icy scent of pine trees that sneaked through the walls. Sometimes grace is a ribbon of mountain air that gets in through the cracks.

I practiced concentrating between each wave of nausea, the way I did when I was in labor, savoring ice chips and apple juice between contractions. Miles from home, holed up deeply alone in a smelly hut, I had the old, familiar feelings of separation: from myself, from God, and from the happy, pretty people outside.

I thought of the woman from the ski patrol, with her small brown eyes. She looked like the monk seals that swim ashore in Hawaii to rest on the sand. The adult seals are six and seven feet long, and they all look like Charles Laughton. The newest tourists on the beach think they are dying and need to be rescued, but anyone who has been there even a day knows that they come onshore to rest. Pool workers from the beachside resorts always arrive, with yellow safety tape and traffic cones, to rope off a space for the seals to rest in. The first time I came upon one in the sand, I thought it was trying to make eye contact with me — I was its last, best hope of being saved. It had sand around its eyes and lots of shark scars. My guy Rory, who surfs in Hawaii every year, laughed and explained that the seals are perfectly fine, and when they are rested, they waddle back to the ocean.

This is how I feel about the world much of the time, when I am not feeling too far gone: Things are how they are supposed to be, all evidence to the contrary. Life swims, lumbers across the sand, rests; lumbers, swims, rests.

I lay there on the bench immobilized. If I were a monk seal, I could have waddled up into a sitting position, slid off the bench, and pulled myself by my flippers back into the ocean. Rory once saw a mother monk seal teaching her pup how to rest by swimming up onto the sand for a while before slipping back into the waves. The two of them practiced over and over, then disappeared into the water. Remembering this made me miss Sam terribly. I felt discarded, and I needed for time to pass more quickly. I would be fine with life's contractions if they would simply pass when I am ready for them to, so I can be okay again and remember what, after all, I'm doing in labor. Being human can be so dispiriting. It is a real stretch for me a lot of the time.

I put my nose to a crack in the wall so I could smell the pine.

I couldn't wait any longer for the ski patrol woman to come back. Where was she? She'd said. She was my only real friend, and I was such a mess. Her voice was gentle and kind — "O that today you would hearken to His voice," the psalmist wrote, and "harden not your hearts." Okay, fine, I said to God, and then noticed that I was much less of a frozen mess than I'd been earlier. This was a lot. I could have sat up, but I wanted the ski patrol person to see the full extent of my suffering — if she ever in fact returned.

I thought of the people I know from church and political circles who are doing a kind of psychic ski patrol in the world, noticing when people are in trouble, refusing to look away, offering an ear and their own warm gloves to wear.

Twenty minutes later, my ski patrol woman did come back, rubbing her bare hands together. "How you doing?" she asked. At first the enthusiasm in her voice worried me, because she sounded as if we might now move on to calisthenics. Then I could tell that she knew I was fine, better, rested. I was peaceful: she was my own private pool-worker, my own mother seal. I sat up and breathed in the fresh air from the open door.

She gave me another Dixie cup of water, and I hoisted it Germanically.

She walked over to the heater and checked my gloves. "They're all ready to wear again if you'll give me mine back."

I stood up. I felt like my old self, which is to say creaky but okay.

"I'd take the chair down," she said. "Unless you really want to ski."

I really wanted to ski. I'd already had one great run down this slope.

She made a huge fuss over me when I left, as if I'd been in an avalanche. I pulled on my gloves and headed out onto the huge white ocean of ice. I glided and fell and got back up and skied little by little, the very best I could, all the way down the mountain.

WAILING WALL

There was so much bad news this winter that many of us were left feeling pummeled and disturbed. Parents and relatives died, kids got into much more serious trouble, and way too many friends got a bad diagnosis. What can you say when people call with a scary or heartbreaking prognosis? You say that we don't have to live alone with our worries and losses, that all the people in their tide pool will be there for them. You say that it totally sucks, and that grace abounds. You can't say that things will be fine down the road, because that holds the spiritual authority of someone chirping "No worries!" at Starbucks, or my favorite, "It's all good!" at the market. It's *so* not all good. And I'm worried sick.

It's fine to *know*, but not to say, that in some inadequate and surprising ways, things will be semi-okay, the way wild flowers spring up at the rocky dirt-line where the open-space meadow meets the road, where the ground is so mean. Just as it's fine to know but not say that anger is good, a bad attitude is excellent, and the medicinal powers of shouting and complaining cannot be overestimated.

One intensely green spring morning, I prepared to teach children at my church about the Wailing Wall in Jerusalem. I had been assigned to teach the youngest children, who have the attention span of squirrel monkeys, but at least I had good curriculum materials and my friend Neshama to help.

I'd been pumped up about the lesson the night before, when I saw an art project suggested in the curriculum materials that involved building a paper Wailing Wall with students, to teach them about pouring one's heart out to God and about letting go. I'd also printed images from the Internet of men clustered at the wall, crowds milling around nearby, harder-to-find shots of women at the wall, multiple copies of one block of stone, and a picture of a young boy and his father in yarmulkes, pushing prayers written on paper into cracks in the wall. This is something I do all the time, shove bits of paper with prayers and names on them into desk drawers, little boxes, my glove compartment. I've found that when you give up on using your mind to solve a problem — which your mind is holding on to like a dog with a chew toy — writing it down helps turn off the terrible alertness. When you're not siphoned into the black hole of worried control and playing fretful Savior, turning the problem over to God or the elves in the glove compartment harnesses something in the universe that is bigger than you, and that just might work.

So I started off class as I always do, by separating the known offenders, two brothers who are four and five and from whom one can expect more or less muffled explosions. We had only boys that day — the brothers, two six-year-olds, and a three-year-old wild man we'll call Frederick — and Frederick's mother.

Each boy reminded me of Sam at different ages, and as he still is: goggle-eyed and watchful at three; at four, newly articulate, like the younger of the two brothers, his eyes big-mammal wide and brown. Sam was still cuddly at that age, more like a baby than a kid, still seeking comforting things — me, for instance. At five, he was like the older of the brothers; he grew more wiry, was prone to anger, and since other children messed with him more, he could no longer afford to space out. He no longer got distracted by his navel, no longer twisted his fingers into his forehead. He and his friends were learning to pick on one another and play the social angle. At five, there's a gap between who you want to be and who you are. You're still pretty small, not able to read or write too well; I know it was scary for Sam to think that he would never learn. Six-year-olds, like the boys visiting, seemed as worldly and independent as bachelors to Sam when he was five. Six-year-olds could ride their bikes to school, and they had a cover — mannerisms to mask how needy and angry and afraid life made them feel much of the time. They were making images of themselves. It's scary when the self divides into one being who will be more noticed and admired, and another, worried person who gapes out at the world from inside.

I welcomed everyone, made introductions, and then launched into Soft Body. We clenched our fists, our faces, and scrunched our shoulders up to our ears, like Nixon. We held that for a minute, grimacing, and at the count of three, we released. Then we did it again. It's a tool for the children, the tool of having their bodies be quiet for a few minutes. Afterward they revert to form

— bouncing in their seats, poking, blurting, sliding down wide-eyed like corpses beneath the table. But when I said, "Butts on chairs! Now!" they obeyed. Except for Frederick, who shimmied and babbled.

His mother looked as if she could use a nice refreshing martini.

Next, as always, we did Loved and Chosen.

I sat on the couch and glanced slowly around in a goofy, menacing way, and then said, "Is anyone here wearing a blue sweatshirt with Pokémon on it?" The four-year-old looked down at his chest, astonished to discover that he matched this description — like, What are the odds? He raised his hand. "Come over here to the couch," I said. "You are so loved, and so chosen." He clutched at himself like a beauty pageant finalist. Then I asked if anyone that day was wearing green socks with brown shoes, a Giants cap, an argyle vest? Each of them turned out to be loved and chosen, which does not happen so often. Even Neshama — Anyone in red shoes today? — leapt toward the couch with relief.

My Jesuit friend Tom once told me that this is a good exercise because in truth, *everyone* is loved and chosen, even Dick Cheney, even Saddam Hussein. That God loves them, because God loves.

"This — more than anything else — does not make sense to me," I said.

"Because you are a little angry," Tom explained. "But when people die, they are forgiven and welcomed home. Then God will help them figure out how to clean up the disgusting messes they have made. God has skills and ideas on how to do this."

After Loved and Chosen, I did a shakedown and made them hand over everything in their pockets that might distract them — or me. We lit a candle: Let there be light, warmth, and all that. No harm in this, right? No worries! We bowed our heads in prayer, our hands to our chins, because in all pictures since time began, good children pray in this pose.

The hardest part came next, when I tried to get the boys to sit quietly for a story from the Bible. I don't want them to feel sentenced to Sunday school: I want, if nothing else, for them to relax their bodies, remember that they are loved and chosen, and hear a great story, because that is how they seem to learn best.

The kids love stories that involve dead people. It's one of the spiritual dimensions that they desperately need to have addressed, the incomprehensible fact that someone is there, and then is not. How can this possibly be, and how can you go on without the dead person? I don't have an answer. There are deaths I've not gotten over yet; but somehow, over time, the acute helplessness of death has become merely painful.

I read them a short version of the story of King David establishing his throne in Jerusalem so that the people of Israel finally had a home in a great city, after the chaotic nomadic life they'd always been living. Before, they'd had to carry the sacred Ark of the Covenant around like so much camping gear. And David's son, wise King Solomon, built a temple.

This was where the Jews flocked to worship. It was supposed to help them stay focused on God and turn their attention away from the distractions outside, and from the idols of the surrounding nations. It was a place where God could hear the cries and prayers and joys of His people, a place of refuge. It was supposed to last forever. Four hundred years later, though, bad guys came from the north, the warriors of King Nebuchadnezzar, and destroyed it, capturing or killing all the Jews they could.

I paused to look at the class: two of the

boys looked utterly undone, the rest looked stoked.

"But one great wall remains to this day," I said. "It's the wall in this one photo, where the boy and his father are sticking a prayer into the cracks. I want you to try to feel a connection between yourselves and the children who came to the wall in ancient times, asking God for help, trusting in His love."

The kids listened pretty well, except for Frederick, who moved sneakily around the room like an incompetent spy. I guided him back to his mother's lap. I wanted to whisper something to him that I'd seen on a bumper sticker that week: that only *one* six-billionth of this was about him. But the lesson was on Letting Go: so I gritted my teeth winsomely.

"What does letting go mean?" I asked. The boys looked around at one another, worried as cats. "Let me show you," I said, and gripped two colored markers, one in each hand. "What if, when we go in for our snacks, someone offers me a juice box, and I won't let go of these pens, even though I'm thirsty." I told them to watch, and you'd have thought I was doing a magic trick as I slowly unfurled my fingers and let the markers drop.

We all thought hard about this. "So why would you *want* to let go?" I asked.

One of the six-year-olds answered, "Because you're thirsty?"

"Bingo!" I cried. Thank you, Jesus! This was suddenly the most successful class I'd ever taught. "See, sometimes, if you're lucky, you get to a point where you're sick of a problem, or worn down by tinkering with it, or clutching it. And letting it go, maybe writing it down and sending it away, buys you some time and space, so maybe freedom and humor sneak in — which is probably what you were praying for all along."

Then I put the supplies on the floor. Frederick grabbed at a pair of safety scissors, and after I took them away, I sent him to his mother and got down on the floor beside my materials. He began to cry, and just like that the center stopped holding, and one of the six-years-olds, horsing around, fell out of his seat and landed on my head. I shouted in surprise, because he'd hurt my neck. After a moment, I realized I was fine, but I turned the class over to Neshama and went outside to compose myself.

I dropped my chin to my chest and rubbed my neck. I felt like a weed, like one of those orange flowers that have sprung up lately, bowed like fiddlehead ferns, and underneath resembling beautiful Chinese dragons: Grrr.

Finally I looked up, at my church. I needed the grown-up service *so* badly, the singing, the prayers, the silence, and especially the very low incidence of injury. Sometimes it's as still as a forest, sometimes a person speaks words of wisdom and comfort, and no one in twenty-one years has hurt me. The music moves you along, you rise and you sit and rise and sing and float, and you open your mouth and let the sound come out. No matter that you may sing poorly, and fumble around with the hymnal, and sing the wrong words, the hymn expands to make room for all the voices, even yours.

We clap a lot at my church — it punctuates the air and chases the devil away. So I took a deep breath, stepped back into the classroom, and clapped for attention.

I passed around the pictures of people at the Wailing Wall that I'd printed. I showed the boys the moss and grass growing in the cracks, and the prayers on paper sticking out. I let them study these, and then I explained that we were going to build a wall for the people of our church, where they could scribble notes to God to help them let go.

We all got down on the floor together. I handed out paper replicas of the limestone blocks that make up the wall, gray, brown, and sand-colored. We crumpled them up to make them more realistic, and stomped on them to burn off excess energy. I gave everyone safety scissors, even Frederick.

I got a piece of poster board, and the greatest invention in the history of Sunday schools everywhere — glue sticks.

We pasted our blocks to the poster board, and taped on strips and wads of green construction paper to represent the wonder of vegetation breaking through the cracks. Then we wrote, right on the blocks, the names of people we loved who were suffering — grandparents, people in nations at war — and then the names of new babies and of pets who had died. While we worked, we had wailing and muttering practice.

I asked Neshama whether she had anything to add about letting go. She put down her glue stick and said, "Maybe turning things over is not the solution to everything, but . . ." She shrugged Hasidically. "You do what you can. Then you get out of the way, because you're not the one who does the work."

How much of the lesson did the children take in that day? I can't answer that, and besides, I wasn't in charge. But it all comes to dropping a few seeds on the ground. If the soil is ready, the seeds will grow, and if not, you could have the Archangel Michael buzzing around the room in a thong and the kids still won't get it. At any rate, we all ended up on the floor with our butts in the air, like ducks feeding in the shallows of a marsh.

DANCE CLASS

One night recently, Neshama and I agreed to be helpers at my friend Karen's special-ed dance class. Neshama wanted to go because she is a lifelong dancer — modern, ballet, Bolinas tribal stomp. Perhaps some of you caught her act during the sixties, when she performed at a nightclub doing the Hippie Dance of Love. She is short, sixty-five, with fuzzy hair like mine. We've been friends since I was twenty-one and drinking heavily, in Bolinas, where we both lived. I am forty-eleven now, sober twenty years, and have moved ten miles away, to another small, tie-dyed town closer to San Francisco.

One thing I love about Neshama is that, like Karen, she is willing to try anything that affords you the opportunity to shake up the Etch A Sketch of everything you suppose is true, a chance to question all your secret opinions: that this thing is good, that one is bad; that this person is better, that one is worse. I truly — or at least sort of — believe that we are all family, created of the same stuff, and that what is true for one of us is true for most of us. I pretend to believe that deep down, Donald Rumsfeld is just as innocent in God's eyes as a newborn: I think my believing in his innocence should count for something — if not for full credit in heaven, then at least a few bonus snack coupons. At the same time I secretly believe that God must love people with developmental disabilities much more than He loves people like me or Rumsfeld, because they are more innocent, and did not bring their problems down on themselves.

And yet, having confessed this, I know that humans want and need exactly the same thing: to belong, to feel safe and respected. I also know that we don't live long. And that dancing almost always turns out to be a good idea. Rumi wrote, "Whatever there is, is only He, / your footsteps there in dancing: / The whirling, see, belongs to you, / and you belong to the whirling." I'm not any good at dancing, but Karen, in Coyote Trickster mode, got me to show up by promising I'd get to be a helper.

So there I was in dance class. There were eighteen adults, of various ages and degrees of disability, in the room at the rec center. I had seen many of them before, at the Special Olympics, bagging groceries at Safeway, and on the streets of Marin, alone at bus stops or walking together. They wore the most tragically terrible clothing you could imagine, plaids coordinated with paisleys and bright florals, like wild and crazy guys. Karen introduced Neshama and me as that evening's helpers, and everyone murmured and hummed and exclaimed, "The helpers!" They came to shake our hands or to stare at us close-up, with awe. You'd have thought Paula Abdul had arrived. Some of them told us their names, and several asked if we were going to dance.

"Yes," Neshama responded, although I had assumed I might help in a more ministerial way.

Many people with Down's syndrome look like family, like relatives of one another, while autistic people look more like the rest of us, if a little tense. Within ten minutes, I discovered that when I spoke to the people in dance class, the veil of illusion kept dropping — the ones who looked most like "the rest of us" were often the least available for ordinary human contact, while the ones who looked seriously different were often the most responsive and engaged. One of the two prettiest women seemed very high-functioning, in a bossy, controlling way, while another pretty one seemed to be hanging in an invisible hammock strung between here, and, well, there. Karen had warned me that you had to keep your eyes on one very shy, spherical Down's-syndrome woman, who'd earned a reputation for performing dances that began innocently but degenerated into cartoonishly lewd stripteases. Once, at Christmastime, she'd gotten down to her undies while grinding along to Brenda Lee's version of "Jingle Bell Rock." But hey, who hasn't?

We formed a circle and introduced ourselves again to the people around us, formally, as if we were about to square dance, do-si-do. Handshakes were mannerly and respectful — it was like being presented to grateful visitors from another planet: "You have come all this way. I take your hand, I look you in the eye. We come in peace." One of the men was huge and reminded me of somebody behind a butcher counter: sweaty, with a mustache disorder, a big gut, a baseball cap. Another wore a Giants T-shirt he had obviously mended himself, with a frayed rope over it, like a confused belt. A number of the people reminded me of sober men and women who once helped me, or people whom I've tried to help, but with a lot fewer tattoos.

I'm not comparing the hardship of being developmentally disabled to that of being an alcoholic or a drug addict, but in dance class, I noticed all sorts of parallels: the off-rhythm gait, the language you can't quite catch, the lack of coordination, the odd affects — too friendly or too far away — the bad teeth, the screwed-up relationships or no relationships at all, the not-fitting-in-ness. It's incredibly touching when someone who seems so hopeless finds a few inches of light to stand in and makes everything work as well as possible. All of us lurch and fall, sit in the dirt, are helped to our feet, keep moving, feel like idiots, lose our balance, gain it, help others get back on their feet, and keep going.

After introductions, we did wiggly warm-up stretches to classic James Brown, and when the music ended, everyone in the circle spun around like the Godfather of Soul, while screaming, "Aaawwhhhooo-hhh." I was pretty good at this. So was a young woman with cerebral palsy, spinning in a wheelchair, grinning, her twiggy fingers curled into somehow sweet claws. The stretches were hard for the heavier dancers, which was about half the class. They struggled like beautiful, ungainly marine

mammals, with short limbs and uncoopera-
tive bulges. But in wiggling, all people shine.

Then it was time for sharing.

We sat in a circle and were invited to share
only one thing about ourselves: Karen had
told me that she'd recently had to add this
"only one thing" rule to put an end to long
gossipy stories, some of which were hatchet
jobs on other people who were present in
the room. She invited everyone to share sad
or scary stuff with her privately, after class.
Most people talked about their relatives,
sometimes angrily — *"No, my niece still can't
speak yet because she is only eight months
old!"* — and sometimes with pride: "My
nephew graduated from high school Satur-
day, and now he is going into the Marines.
And he'll be in charge!" They acted a lot
like my relatives: interrupting and bossing
one another, listening, jostling, showing off,
arguing, trying to get extra attention. A
number begged to share *"just one more
thing."* Some of them were willing to make
exceptions, cut people a little slack. Others
grew sullen, or were on the verge of tears
with worry when people didn't stick to the
rules.

It turned out that most of them attend
Weight Watchers together every week, and
this was another One Thing they wanted to

share, either with elation — "I lost one pound!" — or tearfully — "I gained one-point-three pounds." It made me laugh about my own bad dieting days, like, say, my thirties. I know how it feels. During the worst of it, if I discovered that I had gone from 140 to 139.6, I felt triumphant; if the opposite happened, panic rose in my throat, and I had to stuff it back down with food.

I will never know how hard it is to be developmentally disabled, but I do know the sorrow of being ordinary, and that much of our life is spent doing the crazy mental arithmetic of how, at any given moment, we might improve, or at least disguise or present our defects and screw-ups in either more charming or more intimidating ways.

With half an hour left, it was time for the actual dance instruction. I thought it would be like doing the hokey-pokey, but there were some tricky moves. The first was kick-ball-pivot, which has nothing to do with playing kickball, but is a modern dance step. First you kick one foot, then put the ball of that foot on the floor. Then you do a pivot turn. It's surprisingly hard. I couldn't do it right. I cheated. I just turned. My entire childhood flashed before my eyes: trying and failing to learn cheerleading moves, water ballet, chemistry.

Mercifully, Karen announced it was time for the electric slide, a version of a line dance you might see in bars or on reruns of *Soul Train.* You begin by tapping your feet three times — which I was good at. Excellent, really. Then the Raisin Bran scoop, where you scoop the air twice. Then some wiggles, and a pivot turn — that infernal pivot turn! Then you move forward, everyone together, pushing the air as if clearing a path, backing up to where you started, quacking, for some reason. Then . . . the pivot turn. Tap, scoop, wiggle, pivot, turn, push, quack, pivot.

The magnificence of the dance is in their faces.

We sat down in a circle again, so people could do solos or ensembles in the center. The first solo was by the woman with cerebral palsy, who during the group practice had done great swooping turns in her wheelchair. For her solo, she sat smiling ecstatically and twitched her gnarled hands in time to the music. She was great. So was the music, a Congolese song called "Soweto." The next dancer, an older woman, earnestly counted her every step out loud, evidently unbothered that none of the steps coincided with the music, her jaw set with a determination that bordered on hostility. Then a blonde woman with Down's syndrome performed what I at first thought were gymnastics: a somersault that pretty much got away from her, and a unique cartwheel — palms flat on the floor, then rocking back onto her bottom, then falling over sideways — and then jumping up and down in a one-legged crouch. Karen later told me that this was intended to be break-dancing, a weekly performance by the woman's alter ego, Homegirl from the 'Hood.

After the solos, ensembles of four or five did the Electric Slide together. I joined in with one group. I was great; everyone said so.

And then it was time to go. People shook our hands and thanked us. The gymnast gave me a hug with her head pressed into my waist. Neshama and I left feeling elated and surprisingly tired. It had been only an hour, but it was an immersion. It went deeper than I had thought.

When Karen and I were hiking a few days later, she told me that after class, one of the dancers had exclaimed, "I liked those old ladies! They were helpers, and they danced." These are the words I want on my gravestone: that I was a helper, and that I danced.

57

■ ■ ■ ■

BODIES

■ ■ ■ ■

The bud
stands for all things,
even for those things that don't flower,
for everything flowers, from within, of self-
    blessing;
though sometimes it is necessary
to reteach a thing its loveliness,
to put a hand on its brow
of the flower
and retell it in words and in touch
it is lovely
until it flowers again from within, of self-
    blessing;
as Saint Francis

put his hand on the creased forehead
of the sow, and told her in words and in
    touch
blessings of earth on the sow, and the sow
began remembering all down her thick
    length,
from the earthen snout all the way
through the fodder and slops to the spiri-
    tual curl of the tail,
from the hard spininess spiked out from
    the spine
down through the great broken heart
to the sheer blue milken dreaminess spurt-
    ing and shuddering
from the fourteen teats into the fourteen
    mouths sucking and blowing beneath
    them:
the long, perfect loveliness of sow.

— Galway Kinnell
"Saint Francis and the Sow"

THE MUDDLING
GLORY OF GOD

We moved into our current house six years ago, when Sam was ten. In the old house, our bedrooms had been very close, but in the new place, we were separated by two rooms and two short hallways. He started coming into my room in the middle of the night, curling up on my bed with his own blanket. I tried the obvious ways of helping him get his confidence back — a night-light, bribes, Power Ranger sheets. Nothing worked.

Finally, Sam and I came up with a solution: The first night, he put his sleeping bag and pillow right beside my bed, where our old dog, Sadie, could peer out at him tenderly. The second night we moved the sleeping bag three feet away, to the foot of my bed. The next night, he moved three more feet away. On the fourth night, he made it to the door. He slept there two nights before he was able to put his sleeping bag in the hall. I kept the door open.

"Are you okay?" I called to him in the dark.

"Yeah," he said, in his small but manly voice. The short hallway to the living room took three nights to master. Then there were four nights in the living room, as he crept overland closer to his own room, with four three-foot scootches, one stall, and one night when he had to drag his sleeping bag back three feet. Sometimes he would call out, "Good night" again to hear my voice. There was one valiant worried night in the hall between my study and his room.

"See you tomorrow, Mom."

"Love you, Mom! Doing okay out here, Mom."

A few times he called for me to come sit with him. My nearness lifted him. Sometimes grace works like water wings when you feel you are sinking.

And then, at last, he spent his first night in his spooky new room, bravely, on the floor.

That's me, trying to make any progress at all with family, in work, relationships, self-image: scootch, scootch, stall; scootch, stall, catastrophic reversal; bog, bog, scootch. I wish grace and healing were more abracadabra kinds of things; also, that delicate silver bells would ring to announce grace's arrival. But no, it's clog and slog and scootch, on the floor, in silence, in the dark.

I suppose that if you *were* snatched out of the mess, you'd miss the lesson; the lesson is the slog. I grew up thinking the lessons should be more like the von Trapp children: more marionettes, more dirndls and harmonies. But no: it's slog, bog, scootch.

Until a few weeks ago, I had been scootching along pretty well for a while in size-ten pants, having lost a little weight, feeling I'd nailed the food and weight and body-image business, when all of a sudden my foot met air, and I was unmoored. Within minutes, I was on the edge of full-on food binge, assault eating. I couldn't even remotely find my way back to the path that I'd relied on for the past fifteen years, the path of feeding myself when I am really hungry, trusting my own appetite, and staying at the same weight without too much painful obsession. I was starving, and nuts.

I prayed for God to help me find my way out, and what I heard was, "Call a friend." But something edgier was speaking more loudly, and I pricked up my ears at the sound, even though an old man at church once told me *never* to give the devil a ride. Because if he likes the ride, pretty soon he'll want to drive. It felt as if someone determined and famished had taken the wheel.

I tried doing what usually works when I'm lost: lifting my eyes off my feet and looking around for any clues that might help me get oriented, like the moss on trees, which supposedly tells you which way is north.

And I did discover an important clue — that whenever I want to either binge or diet, it means that there is some part of me that is deeply afraid. I had been worrying about Sam more than usual, and only partly because he had just begun to drive. I had been worried sick about Bush for five years now. There was a terrifying epidemic of breast cancer in my county; like so many others, I had friends who were trying to survive. And lately I'd fallen back into my old habit of acting like classroom helper to the world, doing too many favors for people, at the expense of writing, rest, and gyroscopic balance. I had been to a funeral. I had had a molar pulled. I had recently seen the skin on the back of my neck under fluorescent lights in a hotel mirror. I hadn't seen it in years; now it looked like it was upholstered in a few inches of the Utah desert. Everything was too much.

All I could think to do was what every addict thinks of doing: kill the pain. I don't smoke or drink anymore, am too worried to gamble, too guilty to shoplift, and I have always hated clothes-shopping. So what choices did that leave? I could go on a strict new diet, or conversely, I could stuff myself to the rafters with fats, sugars, and carcinogens.

Ding ding: we have a winner.

I got in the car and headed to Safeway.

It had been a while since I'd had a Safeway apple fritter, but all of a sudden, this was what the thing driving really wanted. A perfect fritter, in the classic tradition, a Frisbee-size patty of deep-fried dough, crisp and crunchy around the edges, doughy in the center, covered with a sugar glaze that makes me think of the Sherwin-Williams logo, the can of paint being poured over the globe. I used to eat fritters in mass quantities, as the Coneheads would have enjoyed them, back when I binged and purged. Then, in early sobriety, I'd snack on them sometimes, because your body craves a replacement for all the sugar you once got in alcohol. Since then, I'd buy one every so often, the way a regular healthy person does, because for no particular reason I'd want one. But this time I went to Safeway and bought all sorts of healthy decoy foods; then I slunk over to the bakery.

And they were out of fritters.

In the history of Safeway, it has never once run out of apple fritters. I understood instantly that God was doing for me what I could not do for myself. I did not turn to the doughnuts, the bear claws, the Danish; I was not hungry for those. I had not been attacked by random lust for just any old sugar-and-petroleum product.

I put all the decoy foods back, left the store, and drove to another market. On the way over, the person at the wheel said, It's not that big a deal. *Anyone* would understand if you binged every so often.

I asked nicely, Now, who exactly is "anyone" again?

Anyone.

I knew this was true. Even Jesus would, although somehow I don't see him ripping open a package of Hostess Ding Dongs for me. But thinking of him reminded me that food would not fill the holes or quiet the fear. Only love would; only my own imperfect love would.

I hate this.

I felt like the man in the joke who has fallen halfway down a cliff and is hanging on by a vine, who calls out for God to save him. God says, "Just let go, my son. I'll catch you." The man thinks about this for a minute and then yells out, "Is there anyone else up there?"

And there was: the thing that was driving. Instead of using my cell phone to call a trusted friend, I continued to the second store, where I bought three apple fritters. Also, a pint of Ben & Jerry's New York Super Fudge Chunk and some Cheetos. Sam loves them, I would say, and it was true. And I got some jalapeño poppers, deep-fried and oozing melted cheese. Mint Milanos. Sara Lee chocolate-dipped cheesecake bites. My mother loves them, I would say; and she did, before she died.

After I paid, I got in the car and took my first bite of fritter, and it was good, the perfectly crisp sugar glaze on the outside, and I nibbled off all the toes of crispness that stuck out, like Kliban's folksinging cat who loved to eat them mousies. I nibbled the outside inch of the first fritter until I hit the doughy center, and then I nibbled the tiny toes off the second one, and the outermost ring. And then, as I pulled into my driveway, the crisp little toes of the third.

The first spoonful of the New York Super Fudge Chunk was more than good: it was *excellent.* So were the next ten, the next twenty. By thirty, though, I couldn't really taste much, so I took a break. Then I moved on, to the Mint Milanos. And they were good. Especially the top four cookies in their little paper panties; especially dipped in milk.

I was so lost. I couldn't follow the bread crumbs back to the path of mental health, because I'd eaten them all. So I ended up eating junk, off and on, until bedtime. I can hardly describe how I felt when it was over: like a manatee alone in an aquarium.

It is hard to remember that you are a cherished spiritual being when you're burping up apple fritters and Cheetos.

I brushed my teeth and stretched out on the bed, and prayed just to feel semi-okay again. I initially felt shame at praying for such a stupid thing, when people all over and in my own life are struggling to survive the end of their worlds. Big surprise: nothing happened. I was in a traffic jam of thoughts. My pastor, Veronica, says that believing isn't the hard part; waiting on God is. So I stuck with it and prayed impatiently for patience, and to stop feeling disgusted by myself, and to believe for a few moments that God, just a bit busy with other suffering in the world, actually cared about one menopausal white woman on a binge.

Back in bed, I remembered an old sermon of Veronica's in which she said that when we are with other people, they should be able to see Jesus' love in our faces, his tender-compassion in our hands. Sometimes I think that Jesus watches my neurotic struggles, and shakes his head and grips his forehead and starts tossing back mojitos. The bad driver certainly whispers this to me. But this time, I decided to fake it and pretend that I had believed what Veronica said, and respond to myself as gently as I would to you; this is all I am ever really hungry for. I got myself some cool water, a pair of soft socks: scootch, scootch. Then waves of nausea and self-loathing, back-track, bog. I thought of all the times my friends have given off light in the darkness, by their generosity, by trying to help in the world, by simply making it through the hard patches with a little dignity, so that other people could see that this could be done. So I was simply kind to myself, and I scootched. I burped my terrible Cyclops burps, which brought such relief that I finally remembered who I was: one of the sometimes miserable all-of-us. I was a soul, not a faulty digestive system. Not a bad neck; not my ruckles and wrinkles and pouches. A woman with a few small, unre-solved issues.

When I remembered that, I was finally

able to call a couple of friends.

I told them that I was lost, and fat, and had once again, in trying to give myself comfort, turned to the wrong thing. That I'd been bingeing all day.

Oh, honey, they both said. Oh, bubbie. How can we help you?

Telling helped a little. It felt as if maybe the worst was over. "But why didn't my faith protect me?" I asked one friend.

"It did," my friend pointed out. "You found your way out of danger — and disgust — through humility, and even confession — to the love of safe people. Now you are safe again."

This was true. I had been in such a toxic pond. But I wanted my faith to be an edifice that I could run to. Strong, clean, pure. A mighty fortress is our God? *Haha.* Thanks for sharing.

"You're a hero to me," my friend continued. "You struggled through something really miserable. You told the truth, when it's so tempting to cover up and disguise it. You said, 'This is the mess of my life, and I need help.' And now you are being helped."

Grace arrived, like the big, loopy stitches with which a grandmotherly stranger might baste your hem temporarily. When I woke the next morning, I felt more kindly toward

myself. I've been pretty relaxed about food
— mostly — for the last few weeks. The
spirit lifted me and now it holds on lightly,
like my father's hands around my ankles
when I used to ride on his shoulders. In
one of my earliest memories, I see myself
on Halloween, four years old. My older
brother is up ahead with his kindergarten
friends, dressed as a hobo with a burnt-cork
mustache. My father and I are walking past
the school where I will start a year later. I
can see the blacktop of the playground il-
luminated by a streetlight. My father is
holding on to my mask. I am too afraid to
wear it. I am afraid of everything at that age
— the dark, my dreams, sleeping alone,
snakes. And I hate masks, because you can't
breathe right, or see very well through the
eyeholes — I must have still had my wits
about me. But I love my silky costume. I
remember picking it out all by myself, for
the first time ever, at the five-and-dime. It is
black with a white oval on the chest. I am a
panda. We walk along on the scariest night
of all, one of my father's hands holding my
mask, one holding me lightly through the
darkness.

Dear Old Friend

We turn toward love like sunflowers to the sun, and then the human parts kick in. This seems to me the only real problem, the human parts — the body, for instance, and the mind. Also, the knowledge that every person you've loved will die — many badly, and too young — doesn't really help things. My friend Marianne once said that Jesus has everything we have, but he doesn't have all the *other* stuff, too. And the other stuff leaves you shaking your sunflower head your whole life through.

I got a message to call my aunt Gertrud last week. She is not my blood aunt; she and her husband, Rex, were my parents' best friends, our two families like one. She became Sam's grandmother one month after conception: neither of her children decided to have kids. I remind her whenever she nags me about something that I ruined my figure to give her a grandson.

She and I stick together.

Her skin is still beautiful, soft, brown, and rosy. It is like very old deerskin gloves. When she was younger, she had silky chestnut hair, very European, but she let it go gray and then radiant moon-white. She was long-legged and looked great in shorts and well-worn hiking boots. Our families spent many weekends together, on Mount Tamalpais, at Palomarin, on the Bear Valley trail at Point Reyes. She had the total lack of self-pity of many people who have survived war, and high expectations that everyone would proceed without complaint or excess. She was not patient with children who lagged behind on the path; she brought us sandwiches on black bread, and dry, perforated raisin bars to eat by streams and rivers. My father, taking pity on us, brought Cokes and grape sodas, and chubs of salami.

Gertrud was also an expert seamstress with great style and taste. She was sort of — what is the word? — cheap, but she accessorized perfectly, at Monkey Wards and Cost Plus. She sewed some things for me over the years, especially as I neared adolescence, so thin that nothing from stores could do justice to my peculiar beauty. She made me two tennis dresses when I was twelve, sky-blue grosgrain trim on one, embroidered cloth daisies on the other; my eighth-grade graduation dress, of periwinkle blue; a hippie shift when I was fourteen, out of an Indian bedspread from Cost Plus; a bigger one when I suddenly filled out, and then some.

My mother and Gertrud raised their kids together, played tennis at the club, fought for left-wing causes, shared a love for cooking and reading, and subscribed to *The Nation* and *The New Yorker.* Our families were at each other's houses all the time. My father and Rex sailed on Rex's boat many weekends, sometimes up the San Joaquin Delta for a whole week. Gertrud was a server, manic and industrious. My mother was a mad little English duchess; people waited on her, in the town where we lived, and then in Hawaii, where she moved when she and my father divorced. Gertrud saved; my mother charged. My mother moved back home broke, ill with diabetes and then early Alzheimer's. Gertrud hovered over her, clucking, mending, fixing things, or trying to.

After surviving breast cancer twice, Gertrud was the one who got dealt the cards to be the survivor, the one who got to see how things came out. One pays an exorbitant price for that honor. A few years ago, my mother died, devastatingly. Five years before that, Gertrud's husband had died of cancer, and twenty years before that, my father. They were the people with whom she had planned to grow old.

Our families are still close, and I am particularly devoted to her. This does not preclude my making a fist at her in public or over meals when she is aggressively stubborn. "That's *enough* out of you, old woman," I thunder, and she shakes utensils in my direction, like a conductor.

Until two years ago, Gertrud was still hiking in the mountains with me and with her other friends, and when you watched her, you could see how much ground she had lost. Even as she had to steady herself with a walking stick while she pointed out alpine wild flowers — crabbing that you should know their names by now — you thought, "*Please* let me look like this at eighty." Then, when you saw her in the convalescent home, frail, pale, defeated, after botched surgery to replace her hip, you thought, "Please don't let me live this long. Please, Jesus: shoot me." But then she resurrected. She came home and set her life in order. She has to rest more than before, but she still lives alone and drives. She keeps up her garden, and she makes us cheesecake for our birthdays. She looks iconic now, shrunken-apple-dollish, small as a child, terribly thin, yet stylish and beautiful.

When her daughter called from Oregon last week, and left me a message that Gertrud was depressed about selling her house, and would I please give her a call, I got on the phone immediately.

I hadn't even known she *was* definitely selling the house. The last I'd heard, she was selling just a parcel of land below the house her husband had built. This was where she had always wanted to die, in this falling-down house where, from the deck, you can see all of San Francisco Bay, Angel Island, Alcatraz, the entire span of the Golden Gate Bridge, the lights of San Francisco, the sailboats, the ferries. Once you could see the railroad yard from it, and the trains, and you could walk a hundred yards to the trestle that took you above the yard to Main Street, until it was all torn down.

For the past few years, Gertrud had spoken about how one day she might need to leave, for some sort of assisted-living apartment, but this was the first I'd heard of her actually selling. We'd all been supportive of her keeping the house forever, but inside we'd hoped that she'd have a nice

cerebral accident before she had to move —
a nice, sudden Hallmark death while dozing.

I called and asked her what was happening. She was distraught. She was going up
to San Rafael at five to sign the papers selling both her house and the parcel of land.
The realtor handling the transaction was
one of Rex's old sailing buddies, and the
buyer, the grown son of childhood friends
of hers from Germany. "I can't talk to you
or anyone now," she told me.

"At least let me drive you there tonight," I
begged.

"No. This is something I need to do
myself. Please pray for me." Now, this
scared me seriously, as Gertrud is a con-
firmed atheist. Her deep spirituality is
absolutely antireligious, rooted entirely in
Nature and caring for people. She has made
her daily rounds all the years I've known
her, taking food and comfort to sick friends.
She was the local head of UNICEF forever.

Still, I have seen an amorphous interest
on her face, during the holiday prayers I
always offer, when I lift up her husband, my
father, my mother. I know she feels the three
of them, then, in a way different from
memory: more like the way you light the
tissue paper that amaretti cookies come

77

wrapped in, stamped with pale pink and blue and green, and make a wish as they flutter on fire into the air, wisps of sparks and then ashes.

I told her I had to leave for an appointment in Berkeley but would call her on my way back to see if she'd changed her mind.

She's very stubborn; really, if you ask me, impossible. The only reason I do not feel like attacking her more often is that she isn't my real mother. But I've come close. Every year when Sam and I take her with us to a writers' conference in the mountains, there are times when I have to leave the living room of our condo to compose myself. Yet she and I will spend hours together happily, reading, making food for Sam and the friends he brings along, cleaning up after; I'll listen to her endless comments, opinions, and questions, and they don't bother me. I'll be a weird old lady someday, too, with opinions on everything, if I live.

Age itself is weird. Everything gets solidified and liquefied at the same time. I honor Gertrud by simply noting her need for constant engagement. But then she'll insist on something that I don't agree with, and in her honeyed voice I'll hear the burr of friendly fascism, which makes me crazy. I'll hear criticism, the hideous drive of the Viennese waltz — "You vill valtz!" — the glittering pleasure of "I told you so." And let's not even get *into* the garbage-eating.

Well, okay, but just briefly. Do all Europeans who survived the war eat garbage? Not simply cutting off half-inches of mold on cheese; I do that. This is the insistence that the bit of toasted bagel that Sam left on his plate yesterday will make a perfectly nice breakfast today — for her.

She's not trying to make me eat it, and still it enrages me.

"Gertrud!" I say. "That is garbage!"

Or I'll come upon her gnawing on an absolutely white cantaloupe rind that she's found on Sam's breakfast plate. Or she'll wrap up overcooked ravioli from yesterday that she wants to take with her, to eat for dinner later. Table scrapings.

But mostly, Gertrud and I find enormous solace in each other. We read the papers together, muttering angrily. She reads Noam Chomsky for pleasure. She brings me great chocolate.

We hike almost every day when we are in the mountains. On our last night up there two years ago, we went stargazing at High Camp, in Squaw Valley. Already at 7,500 feet, we took the gondola up to the meadow where fifty others had gathered to watch a rare Perseid meteor shower. Two astronomers were there to guide us, with powerful telescopes.

Gertrud was the oldest person there, by a good ten years or so. She was wearing a hat, warm clothes, and hiking boots, walking stick in hand, ready for action. You could tilt your head back and see a shooting star every few minutes. Gertrud held on to my arm and leaned back unsteadily.

The astronomers pointed out binary stars we could see with our naked eyes, fuzzy patches they said were stellar graveyards, our old friend the Big Dipper, and Venus, almost below the horizon. We had hiked on this exact spot of land the day before, on a wild flower walk, and the sky tonight was as bright as the field of weedy yellow flowers had been.

Gertrud won't wait in line. Maybe it is a European thing, like the garbage-eating. Maybe she has waited in enough lines to last a lifetime. But I took my turn when she said she was steady enough to stand alone. When I reported that you could see twin stars and stellar graveyards through the telescope, she said rather huffily, "I'll just wait right where I am, and see what I can see."

The stars were as close as berries on a bush.

After a while, Gertrud began to shiver. The night was not that cold, but she is so thin. She teetered as she held on to me, and I stood like a handrail while she got her balance. She held on so tight that it hurt: I could see by the light of the stars and the gondola that her knuckles were white. I rubbed her shoulders briskly, the way you warm up a child just out of the ocean, and we headed down the mountain.

I was thinking of that night when I called her after my appointment in Berkeley, to see whether she wanted me to pick her up after all.

"Yes, please," she said now. When I got to her house an hour later, she was waiting outside, ready for action again: this time, instead of hiking boots, she was wearing a dark blue knit cardigan with gold buttons, and a scarf tucked in around her neck; very nautical, still the admiral of her fleet. She was teary, but composed. All I knew to do was to be willing to feel really shitty with her.

"When did you decide to sell the house?" I asked as we started off.

She said with genuine confusion that she didn't know how it had come to be — she had meant to sell only the parcel of land. A number of friends had convinced her that it made sense to sell both properties now, and rent the house back for a year. This would give her time to find a smaller place, with a garden and a view, and people around to help her in case she fell.

"Couldn't you hire someone to help around the house and drive?"

She said she had changed her mind too many times; had put everybody through too much already, the realtor, the buyer, and her children.

Everything in me wanted to save her — to offer her the extra room in our house, or promise to drop in on her every day. But instead, I did an incredible thing, something I have not done nearly enough in my life: I did nothing. Or at any rate, I did not talk. Miserable and desperate to flee, I listened instead.

Fear and frustration poured out of her as we drove past my entire childhood, past the hillsides that used to be bare, where we slid down the long grass on cardboard boxes, past the little white church on the hill, past the supermarket built on the swamps where we used to raft, past the stores on the boardwalk, on top of which the Christmas star shines every year.

Without particularly meaning to, just before we got on the clotted freeway, I pulled off the road and parked the car in a bus zone.

"Wait a minute, Gertrud. Let me ask you something: What do *you* want to do? What does your heart say?"

She answered after a long moment. "I don't want to sell my house."

"Are you sure?" This was shocking news, and the timing just terrible.

"Yes. But now I have to. I've changed my mind so often."

Neither of us spoke for a minute. "That's the worst reason to do something," I said. She looked at me. "You have the right to change your mind again."

"*Really,* Annie?"

"Yep."

Gertrud looked around with confusion, disbelief, misery. She dried her tears, reapplied lipstick, and picked at invisible lint on her blue knit sweater.

When we pulled onto the realtor's street, she said, "Oh, Annie. This will be such bad news for everyone but me."

"There's a first time for everything," I said. "Besides, your friend can build a nice home for himself on the land."

They were waiting for us when we arrived,

and they managed to be giddy and gentle at the same time. They fussed over Gertrud. These were not men in black capes with twirly mustaches, stealing her house away; they were old friends. After a few minutes of small talk, she looked at the ground. Then she did not look up for a while. Everyone grew quiet, puzzled.

"I've changed my mind," she said, firm, clear, deeply apologetic. "I don't want to sell my house. Only the parcel of land." I held my breath. Old age on a *good* day is a dance we don't know the steps to: we falter. We may not be going in the direction we'd anticipated, or have any clue at all about which way to turn next.

"Gertrud," the realtor asked, "are you *sure?*"

She nodded and said, "Yes, yes," and held on to the arms of her walker so her knuckles turned white, as they had on the night of the meteor shower. Her voice was trembly. I remembered how she'd shivered from the cold. I remembered how one of the astronomers pointed out that the stars were not all one color: there were orange stars, red stars, pale yellow stars. Venus was so close and bright I thought it was a plane, and through the telescope I could see fuzzy cotton balls hundreds of millions of miles away, stellar graveyards, and stellar nurseries, where stars were being hatched.

A Field Theory of Beauty

I woke up from a nap years ago to find my son gazing at me. He took my face into his hands, and peering at me like an old Jewish relative said, "I love that little face."

But I didn't love that little face yet. For too long, and despite what people told me, I had fallen for what the culture said about beauty, youth, features, heights, weights, hair textures, upper arms. Sometimes, in certain lights, I could see that I was beautiful, not in spite of but because of unusual features — funky teeth, wild hair, acne scars. My mother's nose, very English, with pinched indents at the tip and what she called her horns — incredibly helpful to my self-esteem as a child and which I now call my proton nobulators. My father's crooked teeth. Cellulite that would make Jesus weep.

I was forty. My best friend had died two years earlier, at thirty-seven, highly intelligent and pretty. Until she got sick, I'd believed that beauty protected you, surrounded you with a Gardol Shield. Her cancer kicked this belief to pieces. She used to make me wear scarves in my hair, for the burst of color. She'd say, "You have to wear a scarf today, I have cancer." If I protested, she'd say, "It will cheer me up!"

She was so pretty in the scarves and caps she wore to cover her bald head. Many great-looking women in Marin County have lost their hair. At the bank the other day, I ran into an old friend, the Christian Scientist mother of one of my elementary school classmates. She has great polish and style, although she's not exactly pretty. Her hair was gone, replaced by white fuzz, yet she was brimming with health and joy. I said. "Barbara? Are you just finishing up chemo?"

Brightly, she answered, "Oh no, this is something I go through sometimes."

I started comparing notes with her, because on top of having had impossible hair my entire life, now it is falling out. I worry that I will start looking like Richard Nixon with dreadlocks.

"I have a fantastic doctor who helps me with this," she said. I begged for the number and she gave it to me, and it was not until later that I asked myself, Why would you beg for the number of a hair-loss specialist from one of that doctor's bald patients?

It was because she was so beautiful, and she knew and exuded that.

Most of us don't notice how great we look until years, even decades later. Not long ago, I was looking at photos of myself at various ages and weights — way before the neckular deterioration began, way before the fanny pack of menopause — and I could see how gorgeous I must have looked to everyone else. At sixteen, with an Afro, twenty pounds heavier than I'd been the year before, I was radiant with youth, athleticism, and intelligence; at the time, I thought I looked like Marty Feldman. In my mid-twenties, an anorexic hippie, I had a best friend who frequently mentioned that she was the pretty one, which I thought went without saying. But from the pictures I was looking at, I could see that I was the other pretty one, a waifish Renaissance fairy, mesmerizing. Then, at thirty-three, clean, sober, and healing from bulimia, twenty pounds and twenty years lighter than I am now, I'm posing in a periwinkle swimsuit, but covering my thighs in shame, as if someone were photographing me in the junior high locker room instead of on a public beach. There is a rip in the photo; I started to tear it so no one would see.

Twenty pounds ago! Twenty years! Why did it take me so long to discover what a dish I was? And not just because of externals. And how crazy would you have to be, knowing this, yet still not rejoicing in your current looks?

This culture's pursuit of beauty is a crazy, sick, losing game, for women, men, teenagers, and with the need to increase advertising revenues, now for pre-adolescents, too. We're starting to see more and more anorexic eight- and nine-year-olds. It's a game we cannot win. Every time we agree to play another round, and step out onto the court to try again, we've already lost. The only way to win is to stay off the court. No matter how much of our time is spent in pursuit of physical beauty, even to great success, the Mirror on the Wall will always say, "Snow White lives," and this is in fact a lie — Snow White is a fairy tale. Lies cannot nourish or protect you. Only freedom from fear, freedom from lies, can make us beautiful, and keep us safe. There is a line I try to live by, spoken at the end of each Vedanta service: "And may the free make others free."

Of course, some days go better than others.

Let's start with something easy: To step

into beauty, does one have to give up on losing a little weight? No, of course not. Only if you're sick of suffering. Because if you cannot see that you're okay now, you won't be able to see it if you lose twenty pounds. It's an inside job.

I should know: I lost ten pounds last year. Someone who spent $30,000 at a diet hospital told me the secret of how she lost weight there: Eat less, exercise more. Oh, and here's $5,000 worth of cutting-edge advice: Drink more water. So I did that, and in only three months lost ten pounds. You couldn't sell one copy of a magazine by putting this on the cover: "Lose Ten Pounds in Just Three Months." Oh, boy! But it worked, and guess what? No one noticed, as God is my witness, except Sam and my boyfriend and a couple of friends, whom I badgered constantly for assurance that I looked thinner.

Oh, and my tennis partner, who cried out joyfully, "Annie! Have you lost weight? Look how thin your neck is now!"

It's *so* hopeless. What are we going to do? I don't know. But I suppose, while we are on the subject of weight, we might as well address the neck. The neckage.

The situation is deeply distressing: the wattle and the wrinkles that gather like Roman shades. The liver spots. The soft pouch like a frog's vocal sac, or the gular pouches of Komodo dragons that now connect the chin to the neck. But it could be so much worse, as is usually the case, because at least the neck is recessed. God recessed the neck for a loving, caring reason. While the face is right out front, She set the neck back, out of direct light, in the shadows.

Sure, you can still see that gravity is having its say, because the neck is where it all shows — it's like the thighs of the head.

Yet it helps to think of the neck as something — a pedestal, say, or a plinth — on which you'd set a work of art. A stand for the head and the face. The fact that it is not an incredibly attractive stand doesn't matter one bit. It's there to display your face, your eyes — which is where you carry who you are — your intelligence, goodness, humanity, excitement, serenity. Over time, these are the things that change the musculature of your face, as do laughter, and animation, and especially whatever peace you can broker with the person inside.

It's furrow, pinch, and judgment that make us look older — our mothers were right. They said that if you made certain faces, they would stick, and they do. But our mothers forgot that faces of kindness and integrity stick as well.

I have a friend who has a big pancake face and feathery brown hair, with patches of scalp showing. She has peasanty potato features, and she's too tall, and totally inelegant. But she loves her life. She's chosen a life of prayer, service, and travel. She's always in a sort of infuriating state of wonder, of appreciating what is, instead of fretting about what she wishes was. But she's great-looking — everyone thinks so — because of the expressions on her face and the way she looks at you.

She is radiant with spirituality and humor; she was dealt the same basic cards we all were, but somehow she could see that the cards were marked, so she put them down and refused to play. You can't win with marked cards. Refusing to play has left her with hands free to do what really matters to her, what her heart longs to do in this life. Doing those things has made her beautiful. She puts on lipstick, a warm, soft fleece vest, a matching scarf, and she's set, way ahead of the game.

Joy is the best makeup. Joy, and good lighting.

If you ask me, a little lipstick is a close runner-up.

I know women from every place on the

makeup continuum: some who wear none; some who wear a lot, who spackle it on, who could play Shakespeare in the park as soon as they drop the kids off. I know some who wear a lot, and look wonderful.

It's only when you think you need to be concealed, because you're unacceptable, that makeup causes harm. Skin does get rattled with age; wrinkles and hectic color do not contribute to an impression of the dewy calmness of youth. But some makeup, while perhaps not simulating dewy youth, acts as a kind of airbrushing. It restores balance to the face. It makes you look less terminal.

Also, it distracts from the melatonin mustache.

And pretty lipstick makes you look so much less tense and mean. Left to their own devices, lips pucker with the purse strings of age; lipstick can make them soft and more relaxed again.

I wear tinted moisturizer, light blush, and lipstick. It gives me a face I am happier to bring into the world. I look less scary. I'm very glad to claim the crone who is coming to life within me; I just don't want her to screech so loudly that she silences the little girl who is still around, drowns out the naughty teenager, or mutes the flirtatious middle-aged woman.

Here is my theory: I am all the ages I've ever been. You realize this at some point about your child — even when your kid is sixteen, you can see all the ages in him, the baby wrapped up like a burrito, the one-year-old about to walk, the four-year-old napping, the ten-year-old on a trampoline.

We're like Magic 8-Balls. After you ask your question and shake the 8-Ball, you read the answer in the little window. If you ever broke open a Magic 8-Ball with a hammer, you discovered that it contained a many-sided plastic object, with an answer on every facet, floating in a cylinder of murky blue fluid. The many-sided core held the answer to your question. My theory is that, as with our children, as with every surface of that geodesic dome inside the 8-Ball, every age we've ever been is who we are.

So how can I be represented by a snapshot, or any one specific aging age? Isn't the truth that this me is subsumed into all the me's I already have been, and will be?

Anything that helps diminish self-consciousness is a blessing: self-consciousness looks like the other furrows and shadows on our faces, the smudges under our eyes.

The most utterly unself-conscious woman I know is a nun named Gervais. She runs a Catholic school for girls down the road from me. She's close to seventy, but she has the innocence of a girl. If you consider her features, she has a pleasant face. Her hair is short and graying, and she stands tall, in a way that is willowy and flexible, an economy of self-containment and abundance at once, like bamboo. She is plugged into her school and is a do-gooder in the greater community, in touch with everything around her, but she doesn't need anything from it: the plainness and holiness of the world seem enough for her, and this knowledge makes her beautiful.

She has the beauty of modesty, which is a virtue the world doesn't have much truck with: one ordinary flower in a vase, as opposed to a bouquet.

When Jesus was asked about beauty, he pointed to nature, to the lilies of the field. Behold them, he said, and *behold* is a special word: it means to look upon something amazing or unexpected. *Behold!* It is an exhortation, not a whiny demand, like when you're talking to your child — "Behold me when I'm talking to you, sinner!" Jesus is saying that every moment you are freely given the opportunity to see through a different pair of glasses. "Behold the lilies of the field, how they grow; they neither toil nor spin, and yet I tell you, even Solomon in all his glory was not arrayed like one of these." But that's only the minor chord. The major one follows, in his anti-anxiety discourse — which is the soul of this passage — that all striving after greater beauty and importance, and greater greatness, is foolishness. It is ultimately like trying to catch the wind. Lilies do not need to do anything to make themselves more glorious or cherished. Jesus is saying that we have much to learn from them about giving up striving. He's not saying that in a "Get over it" way, as your mother or your last, horrible husband did. Instead he's heartbroken, as when you know an anorexic girl who's starving to death, as if in some kind of demonic possession. He's saying that we could be aware of, filled with, and saved by the presence of holy beauty, rather than worship golden calves.

I saw a woman on the beach in Hawaii three years after my son told me that he loved my little face. I was forty-three, and in the early stages of seeing that I had, in fact, become a woman of beauty: I hadn't fully grown into this yet — I hadn't even met my friend who wears the fleece vests,

or the Catholic nun with the Zen beauty —
but the truth, which bats last, was pressing
through more and more of the confusion
and judgment that had blinded me most of
my life. The woman on the beach, who was
about my age, was playing in the surf with
her young child. She was near the shore, in
water that barely reached her knees, so I
could see her clearly. There was nothing
physically dramatic about her. Nearby in
the water or tanning themselves on beach
towels were younger women and teenagers
in bikinis, who were brown, lithe, smooth,
and perfect, who made you want to kill
yourself. But this woman looked, well, like
us, like me and my friends. She was of aver-
age height, with long, dark hair, a bit heavy,
with the thigh challenge and a poochy
stomach. And she was wearing a bikini, like
all the younger women, whereas I, like the
other women over thirty, was wearing a one-
piece spandex suit, designed for maximum
suckage and disguise. But here she was,
splashing around in a black string bikini,
with an extraordinary lack of self-
consciousness and a glistening confidence.
You couldn't take your eyes off her. She
commanded the beach. Everyone got it —
well, except for a few men.

We sneaked looks at her, as if she were a

movie star. She was the Greek goddess of surf. We beheld her. I thought, "That could be me someday. I could wear a bikini too, theoretically."

Perhaps I wasn't going to buy a bikini anytime soon. But I wondered whether I could splash about like her, with abandon, my head thrown back and my arms held out to the sun. And later that day, I did. Okay: I was wearing mascara, and the same old jaws-of-death swimsuit I'd been wearing that morning. And when I dropped my towel in the sand, I felt shy and stricken and jiggly. After a minute I straightened my shoulders, reached for my son's hand, and ran with him into the ocean, and I splashed and sploshed and ducked under the waves, and then leapt back up to the air, like Our Lady of the Tides, for all the world to see.

■ ■ ■ ■

IN CIRCULATION

■ ■ ■ ■

Your absence has gone through me
Like thread through a needle.
Everything I do is stitched with its color.
— W. S. Merwin,
"Separation"

CHEESE LOVE

After two recent nights in a row of insomnia, I finally got to sleep last Sunday at a reasonable hour, only to be shaken awake at midnight by my son. My first thought was that we had an intruder, and I reached for the tennis racket I keep by my bed in case I need to kill someone. "No, no, Mom, I just can't sleep," Sam cried out plaintively.

"That's terrible to wake *me,* because *you* can't sleep."

"You're my mom," he said. "I'm *supposed* to come to you with my problems."

The first year after my mother's death, I felt a lot of sadness that I had never had a mother to whom I could take my problems. She *was* my problem, or at any rate, this is what I had always thought, and continued to think for a long time. Mothers were supposed to listen and afterward, to respond with wisdom or perspective. But perhaps my mother didn't read her owner's manual.

Mothers were supposed to raise their children in such a way that the children grew up to be responsible, able to participate in life, able to thrive, more or less, both alone and in community. You taught a child to play, for instance, so she could stay healthy and have fun. But my mother so pressured me to be a tennis champion that I had migraines until I quit playing tournaments; she was so competitive that it was ten years before I could even watch Wimbledon with her on TV. And mothers were supposed to teach their kids not to be slobs, and to make their beds in the mornings. A child would thus learn that she was part of an organism, a household where she respected the other inmates enough to pick up after herself, to smooth the bedcovers, removing any socks or books or toys that might leave a discernible bump. But — and I mean this nicely — my mother was a slob, and we were all slobs, until we got sober. My mother's bed always looked like Krakatoa, unless I made it, because she didn't have a clue that you could take care of the inside of things, like friends or your own heart, by tending to surfaces: putting on a little moisturizer, say, or making the bed. Surfaces were strictly for tricking nonfamily into thinking you and your family were enviable, more functional than you were.

The first year after my mother's death, I felt as if the weight of the world had been lifted off me, and ten months later, lighter by twelve trillion pounds or so, I met and fell in love with a cool, decent man. His mother had also died that year, had also been a queenly Englishwoman; had also originally been named Dorothy. His mother went by "Dot"; mine called herself Nikki. I could do a dead-eye impersonation of both of them at once: their imperial madness, their royal kindness, their poise marbled into all that arrogant English self-loathing: the nostrils, the skittish, demanding ways.

During the second year after my mother died, my child became a teenager. I discovered that even reasonably well-adjusted adolescents are often trying to shred your respect, because they are trying to individuate, which is easier when your mother is a total embarrassment, a moron, or both. It seemed natural when I was doing it with my mother, but I tell you, it is wrenching to see it now. I started to understand the existential hollowness she had felt before she had children, the depths of her sorrow when we separated out from her, and how the hollowness threatened to consume her again.

We responded in different ways: She began to work full-time to put herself through law school, then graduated when I was eighteen. I began to put myself down for naps every afternoon. I had an easier time of it than she'd had — although she slept better. I was broke only until my kid was four. She was broke forever.

I was able to scatter her ashes early in the third year after her death. I was able to ache for her, for all that had been so impossible for her to bear, for the bad cards she had been dealt. Yet I could forgive her only about half the time. I was struggling to learn the little things she forgot to teach me — that I was beautiful, and of value, regardless of how well or poorly I was doing in the world — and was mad that she had given me such a lousy owner's manual. I saw her as the foil, and believed that I had grown to be the woman I was simply because of how hard I had to work to defend myself against turning out like her.

When people reminisced about her, I would put my hand to my brow and shake my head slowly. "Ay-yi-yi," I always said, and everyone understood why. They could see why I might have had such a hard time with her, and what a good daughter I had been to take such great care of her anyway.

104

But now, a few years after her death, I can see in my son's eyes so many points I'd missed about her. Her eyes were large and brown, like Sam's, but always frantic, like a hummingbird that can't quite find the flower and keeps jabbing around: she must have been starving to death a lot of the time. I can see in Sam's eyes that he sometimes finds me controlling and annoying — *none* of the other kids have to make their beds — and I realize what superhuman patience it took for my mother to live with kids. I see Sam and me get mad at each other, over and over, but then we apologize, become friends again; I see how each time this is redemption. How amazing it is to share that.

When we have children, we know they will need us, and maybe love us, but we don't have a clue how hard it is going to be. We also can't understand when we're pregnant, or when our relatives are expecting, how profound and dicey it is to have a shared history with a child, shared blood, shared genes, even humor. It means we were actually here, on earth, for a time, like the Egyptians with their pyramids, but with kids, it's an experiment: you wait and see what will come of it, and with people, that almost always means a mess.

And that is what my mother has given me

in the fourth year after her death. I can see now that out of that mess came a bunch of gifts — her generosity in the midst of being broke, even when that meant charging things; and the gift of having a gift for friendships; and the gift of survival, life-forcing her way over the jagged rocks of failure. So many women of her generation were wiped out by the whacking down that life gave them, but my mother mostly stayed one step ahead, until finally, the plaque of Alzheimer's filled her brain. Then, she had children, whom she *must* have raised right, because we entered into that and cared for her.

The other day I found some notes I'd written the summer before she died, when she started calling to tell me she was renting us a great box, with cheese! It was going to be so wonderful. "What box, Mom?" I kept asking, and she'd get furious with herself, and with me. Then she'd call the next day to say she had gotten us the box. With the cheese.

"It's not a box containing cheese?" I asked, thinking Hickory Farms.

"Oh, for Christ's sake," she snapped, and hung up.

When I went to her apartment to investigate, she opened the door and said, "The man brought the box today!"

I stepped inside to see, and there on her television set was a cable box that she'd rented, so she and I could watch Wimbledon together on pay-per-view. Then she flung open the refrigerator door, to show me all the cheese.

At Death's Window

The man I killed did not want to die, but he no longer felt he had much of a choice. He had gone from being tall and strapping, full of appetites and a brilliant manner of speech, to a skeleton, weak and full of messy needs.

He and his wife still loved each other very much, but he'd lost the ability to do the things he had most loved to share during their thirty years together: to cook and overeat, to hike and travel. He had always been passionately literary, but he was losing the ability to read and write, which had defined his life. Both elegant and down-to-earth, with lifelong depression and a rich, crabby sense of humor, he was sixty when he was diagnosed with cancer.

One day he'd been like the rest of us, comically forgetful, trying to live as fully as he could while trying to slow down, and attempting to get through it all without too

much difficulty. Then stomach pain, head-
aches, and like sudden bad weather on vacation, only months to live.

Everyone recommended that he contact a
hospice provider to help with pain manage-
ment, but this was not his way. He said that
if it was just his body deserting him, maybe.
But his mind? His ideas? His self?

Mel and Joanne (that's what I'm going to
call them) told me about it one night over
dinner. Their grown kids wanted Mel to do
chemo; aggressive treatment might buy him
six months, or maybe not, and he had
decided against it. He wanted to feel as well
as he could for as long as he could, savor
his family and friends and the beauty of life,
on his own terms, in the strange basket of
sickness. And if the fear and suffering got
too great? Well, they'd deal with that then.

That night was the closest I came to
drinking in all the years I'd been sober, but
somehow I didn't drink. I believed that God
would be close to us all, no matter how
things bounced, even though Mel was not a
believer. And the following months were a
mosaic of beauty, love, and his body breaking down. He could no longer hike, and he
wasn't ever hungry. He was by turns depressed, fascinated, scared, fine, exhausted,
sad, accepting, enraged, grateful, and

amazed at the love and support that surrounded him. If you have a body, you are entitled to the full range of feelings. It comes with the package.

At first, opiates diminished the pain without muddying his mind, which was as finely tuned as a melancholy thoroughbred's. But then he began to space out a little more often, and he became terrified by the prospects. One day over lunch, I told him that if he ever experienced too much pain or diminishment, I would try to help him die on his own terms, if he wanted.

He was surprised, and so was I. I hadn't particularly planned on offering this. I told him about the evening many years earlier when my brothers and I promised my father we would help him die if his brain cancer took him to a place that he could no longer endure. My father was relieved to the point of tears, but looking over the top of his Benjamin Franklins, he pointed at us sternly and quoted Duke Ellington's great line "Do nothing till you hear from me."

We promised, but when he got to the point where we knew he would not want to be in that shape, he was no longer capable of making difficult decisions. Two months before he died, as he lay in a hospital bed in our one-room cabin, in what amounted to a coma, my younger brother and I crushed up some barbiturates that his doctor had given him to help him sleep. But we couldn't do it. We were too young.

All of his old friends who were part of his final months said sternly that we must not play God, that nature must be allowed to take its course — and they were all atheists. So we did the best we could, and it sucked, and it was beautiful. But the whole time I knew he had not wanted to end up in the shape he did.

I know if the tables had been turned, he would have helped me out.

So I offered to help Mel if he ever needed me. We talked about it briefly. What did I think death was like, he asked. I didn't have a clue, but I'd heard an Eastern mystic say that it was like slipping out of a pair of shoes that had never fit very well. We moved on to what we were reading, and how our kids were. I knew for a fact that Mel believed in assisted suicide. We had discussed a story about it in the paper once: A local man gave his wife an overdose, then sealed her upper body in a plastic trash bag with duct tape. He gave himself an overdose of pills, and they died holding hands. What love!

Mel was somewhat surprised that as a Christian I so staunchly agreed with him

111

about assisted suicide: I believe that life is a kind of Earth School, so even though assisted suicide means you're getting out early, before the term ends, you're going to be leaving anyway, so who says it isn't okay to take an incomplete in the course?

Nothing more was said until some time later, when Mel, Joanne, and I were at dinner. "Annie," Joanne said, "we want to talk about your offer." Oh my God, I thought — I had just been being nice. I couldn't take someone's life. I'm not at all that sort of girl. I'm usually more like a flight attendant — bringing people cool drinks, blotting spills.

"I won't be me for much longer," Mel said. I don't remember what else was said. I asked whether his doctor would prescribe barbiturates — when my father was dying, we had communicated with the Hemlock Society, and I knew exactly how many Seconal pills it took to kill a big person, how to crush them up and add them to applesauce, and how to feed the sick person toast and tea so that he wouldn't throw up the pills.

They shook their heads. They hadn't known their doctor long and felt too shy about asking. Shy!

I didn't know where to start. Usually with life, you start wherever you are, and you flail around for a while — now you just nose around on the Internet, but this was more than a decade ago. You couldn't go around asking any old doctor for a bottle of sleeping pills or painkillers; it just wasn't done. So I did what you had to do in the old days, before computers: I talked to a number of trusted friends.

Through wily, underground ways, I came up with a prescription that would cover enough pills for a lethal dose. One night Mel and I had a cryptic phone conversation. "I got it," I told him, like a spy or a drug dealer.

A month later, Joanne called and asked if I could come to their house the following night. Their best family friend would be with us. I should come around dinnertime. They would have a simple meal for us; there would be toast, tea, and pudding for Mel.

He was in the kitchen when I arrived, very thin and weak, but still definitely Mel. Their friend was there, teary, solemn, and amiable. Joanne had prepared soup for us, with bread and cheese. For the next couple of hours, Mel asked us to put certain CDs on the stereo — Bach, Dylan, Leontyne Price. We shared our favorite stories. He was absolutely clear as a bell, brilliant as ever. We all cried a little, but not at the same time. The air smelled faintly of honey and laundry, and illness.

I remember coming upon a cat once, in tall grass on a hillside near a fire road. It was barely alive. Its eyes were open, and I had to bend in close to see that it was still breathing. I almost picked it up and took it to my vet, but my instincts told me to leave it, that it would be frightening for it to leave the soft grass on which it lay, and the smells of the sun and its own body in the weeds.

Joanne and their friend had wine. Mel had a scotch. We ate in the kitchen. At about eight, Mel looked at Joanne and said he was ready.

The lighting was soft in the bedroom. He went into the bathroom, changed into worn, light blue pajamas, and got into bed, wasted, sad, sweet, and comfortable. The friend and I stood around, or sat nearby. Joanne stretched out on her side of the bed.

Later I went into the kitchen and crushed the pills with a mortar and pestle, and stirred them into applesauce in a tiny Asian bowl.

Mel grimaced when I fed it to him, like a child swallowing medicine. He thanked us, told us how much he had loved his life, and how he wished he could live with us forever. But every person owes God a death, he said, paraphrasing Shakespeare, and everyone should be as lucky as he.

He told us about the presents he had left for each of us. Mine was a framed eight-by-ten-inch photograph of Abraham Lincoln that Mel had kept on the wall in his study, a reproduction of the last picture of Lincoln taken before he was assassinated. There was a crack running across his forehead, from a flaw in the ancient plate. Mel wanted me to be guided in my work by the depth of sorrow and compassion in Lincoln's eyes.

After a while, Mel looked around, half smiled, and fell asleep. The three of us got up to stretch, to get wine or water, to change CDs. Mel breathed so quietly, for so long, that when he finally stopped, we all strained to hear the sound.

THE BORN

Everything was going swimmingly on the panel. The subject was politics and faith, and I was onstage with two clergymen with progressive spiritual leanings, and a moderator who was liberal and Catholic. We were having a discussion before an audience of 1,300 people in Washington, D.C., about many of the social justice topics on which we agree; we were discussing the immorality of the federal budget, the wrongness of the president's war in Iraq . . . Then an older man came to the mike and raised the issue of abortion, and people just lost their minds.

Or at any rate, I did.

Maybe it was the way in which the man couched his question, which was about how we should reconcile our progressive stance on peace and justice with the "murder of a million babies every year in America."

The man who asked the question was soft-spoken, neatly and casually dressed. First

116

Richard, the Franciscan priest, answered that this was indeed a painful issue, but that it was not the only "pro-life" matter with which progressives — including Catholics — should concern themselves during elections. There were also the "pro-life" matters of capital punishment and the war in Iraq, poverty and HIV. Then Jim, the Evangelical minister, spoke about the need to reduce the number of unwanted pregnancies, and the need to defuse abortion as a political issue, by welcoming pro-choice and pro-life supporters to the discussion with equal respect for their positions. He spoke cautiously about how "morally ambiguous" the question was.

I sat there frozen. The moderator turned to me and asked if I would like to respond.

I did: I wanted to respond by pushing over the table.

Instead, I shook my head. I love and respect the Franciscan and the Evangelical, and agree with them ninety-plus percent of the time. So I did not say anything at first.

When I was asked another question, though, I paused. There was a loud buzzing in my head, the voice of reason saying, "You have the right to remain silent," and the voice of my conscience, insistent. I wanted to express calmly and eloquently, that people who are pro-choice understand that there are two lives involved in an abortion — one born (the pregnant woman) and one not (the fetus) — and that the born person must be allowed to decide what is right: whether or not to bring a pregnancy to term and launch another life into circulation.

I also wanted to wave a gun around, to show what a real murder looks like. This tipped me off that I should hold my tongue until further notice. And I tried.

But then I announced that I needed to speak out on behalf of the many women present, including myself, who had had abortions, and the women whose daughters might need one in the not-too-distant future — people who must know that teenage girls will have abortions, whether in clinics or dirty back rooms. Women whose lives had been righted and redeemed by *Roe v. Wade.* My answer was met with some applause, but mostly a shocked silence.

Pall is a good word. It did not feel good to be the cause of that pall. I knew what I was *supposed* to have said, as a progressive Christian: that it's all very complicated and painful, and that Jim was right in saying that the abortion rate in the country was way too high for a caring and compassionate society.

But I did the only thing I could think to do: plunge on and tell my truth. I said that this was the most intimate decision a woman could make, and she made it alone, in her deepest heart, though sometimes with the man by whom she was pregnant, with her dearest friends, or with her doctor — but without the personal opinion of, say, Tom DeLay or Karl Rove. I said that I could not *believe* that men committed to equality and civil rights were still challenging the basic rights of women. I thought about the photo op where President Bush had signed legislation limiting abortion rights, surrounded by nine self-righteous white married males, who had forced God knows how many girlfriends into doing God knows what. I thought of Bush's public appearance with children born from frozen embryos, whom some people call "snowflake babies," and of the embryos themselves, which he called the youngest and most vulnerable Americans.

And somehow, as I was speaking, I got louder and maybe more emphatic than I actually feel, and said that it was not a morally ambiguous issue for me *at all.* I said that fetuses were not babies yet; that there was actually a difference between pro-choice people, like me, and Klaus Barbie.

Then I said that a woman's right to choose was nobody else's goddamn business.

This got their attention.

A cloud of misery fell over the room, and the stage. At last Jim said something unifying enough for us to proceed — that liberals must not treat with contempt and exclusion people who hold opposing opinions on abortion, partly because it was tough material, and partly because we would never win another election.

Not until the reception afterward did I realize part of my problem — no one had told me that the crowd was made up largely of Catholics. I had flown in at dawn on a red-eye, and in my exhaustion and hibernation had somehow missed this one tiny bit of information. I was mortified: I had to eat several fistfuls of M&M's just to calm down.

Then I asked myself: Would I, should I, have given a calmer answer? Wouldn't it have been more useful, and harder to dismiss me, if I had sounded more reasonable, less spewy?

I might have presented my position less stridently, less divisively. But the questioner's use of the words "murder" and "babies" had put me on the defensive. Plus, I was — I am — so confused about why we still have

120

to argue with patriarchal sentimentality about minuscule zygotes, when real, live, already born women, many of them desperately poor, get such short shrift from the government now in power.

Most women like me would much rather use our time and energy fighting to make the world safe and just and fair for the children we do have and do love, not to mention the children of New Orleans and Darfur. I am tired and menopausal and would like for the most part to be left alone: I have had my abortions, and I have had a child.

But as a Christian and a feminist, the most important message I can carry and fight for is the sacredness of each human life, and reproductive rights for all women are a crucial part of that. It is a moral necessity that we not be forced to bring children into the world for whom we cannot be responsible and adoring and present. We must not inflict life on children who will be resented; we must not inflict unwanted children on society.

During the reception, an old woman came up to me and said, "If you hadn't spoken out, I would have spit," and then raised her fist in the power salute. We huddled for a while, and ate M&M's to give us strength.

It was a communion for those of us who
continue to believe that civil rights and
equality and even common sense may
somehow be sovereign one day.

■ ■ ■ ■

Forgivishness

■ ■ ■ ■

It's hard to fight an enemy who has out-posts in your head.
— Sally Kempton
as quoted in Esquire *magazine, 1970*

NUDGES

If my heart were a garden, it would be in bloom with roses and wrinkly Indian poppies and wild flowers. There would be two unmarked tracts of scorched earth, and scattered headstones covered with weeds and ivy and moss, a functioning compost pile, great tangles of blackberry bushes, and some piles of trash I've meant to haul away for years.

I used to create a lot more garbage, and then I got sober twenty years ago. Now I try to clean as I go, because sober people taught me that a willingness to help clean up the mess we've made is a crucial part of adult living; that our scary, selfish, damaging behavior litters the planet. I confess that in my emotional trash heap are some rusty old cans from ten and twelve years ago, when several close friendships broke up irretrievably.

Garbage hardens your heart.

My friend Father Tom says that when we appear before God, God will say, "I love you very much. I forgive you all your crap. Now go clean up your mess, and then come into heaven, because lunch is waiting." I don't want to miss lunch the day they serve Blum's coffee crunch cake, so I finally got to that one pile not long ago.

Just after I got sober, I met a wonderful couple, funny, charming intellectuals. They were spiritual in the same way I was and am, which is to say devout, with a sometimes bad attitude, a black sense of humor, and tendencies toward gossip and character assassination. We hit it off instantly.

They lived in the South, but they both occasionally taught at writers' conferences in California, and I saw them whenever they were in town. Our sons were born a month apart, and two years later, we lost longtime best friends to cancer. We saw each other through.

I was always a little jealous: they had met and married during their senior year in college, where they slipped away for long weekends in bed, drinking scotch and reading *Anna Karenina* out loud. This was almost more than I could bear — to have read Tolstoy out loud to each other. In bed!

Hemingway I could have handled, or beer.

But Tolstoy? And scotch?

Also, they had money. They both worked at universities, and help from their families had bought them a beautiful home with a huge backyard.

I was a renter. A year before she died, my best friend described my house politely as a rattrap, which it was. But it was definitely one of your nicer rattraps, as these things go, with shade trees and a huge sunlit kitchen.

One summer, when our sons were nearly four, the couple invited Sam and me to stay with them at a rental house on the Gulf Coast. They sent us tickets: I did not have any money. The man had gotten a big advance for his second novel, and a vacation at the shore was a dream come true.

We had one of those rare vacations that are as casual as a kitchen: long days in the sand with our sons, swimming, watching sunsets, making meals. We took turns reading the boys to sleep. We were all kind of in love, except for, well, the arithmetic — the two of them, the one of me.

Then, that fall, I noticed during our phone calls that the man was talking about his money perhaps a little more frequently than was strictly necessary. I was barely making ends meet. Besides his big advance, he had a movie deal in the works. He and his wife were thinking of buying a summer house, near the one where we had vacationed. I felt wormy whenever the topic came up. I said all the right things, in my best girl voice, which I like to think drowns out the voice of the snake inside me.

I became the Dickensian orphan, gripping the window, peering in at the happy couple in their big house. I felt so less-than, and so jealous.

At the same time, I wanted to say, "Wouldn't it make more sense for you to discuss purchasing a second home with another home owner? Instead of a rattrap-renting single mother?"

Jealousy always has been my cross, the weakness and woundedness in me that has most often caused me to feel ugly and unlovable, like the Bad Seed. I've had many years of recovery and therapy, years filled with intimate and devoted friendships, yet I still struggle. I *know* that when someone gets a big slice of pie, it doesn't mean there's less for me. In fact, I know that there isn't even a pie, that there's plenty to go around, enough food and love and air.

But I don't believe it for a second.

I secretly believe there's a pie. I will go to my grave brandishing a fork.

When I was young, I used to be so jealous of other girls that it crippled me. I was a good girl, but underneath that plank of sweetness, the worms lived in the moist earth. I didn't know other people were just like me, beautiful and awful, kind and insane. Like all smart kids, I knew where the tunnels and the food were, under that plank, so mostly I did okay, unless something lifted the plank, and then you would see me lying exposed in the light.

When I was ten, I was so jealous of my pretty tennis partner that during a sleepover at her house, after she'd gone to bed, I hid in her closet and splashed water on her catgut racket strings, the best and most expensive kind (my family could afford only nylon), because moisture made the catgut fray.

I grew up and developed some of the skills and wisdom that life gives us. I learned to take myself less seriously, and this helped me panic less. I acquired a little more depth, after seeing enough of life's fluctuations to know that you come through. And I still get jealous.

One day, thirty years after I wet those tennis strings, my writer friend called me to say that he and his wife had bought their summer house. "You'll love it," he told me.

"You've got to come out this summer. We'll send you tickets. Please say you'll come."

I didn't want to go, because I sort of hated him, and me, and wanted to splash water on his strings, or stab one of us in the neck with the pie fork.

"That is so sweet of you, honey," I said. "That's great!" What I meant was: Why do you keep mentioning your multiple houses to me, you asshole?

I couldn't help noticing that I had crossed a line.

"They can come!" he called to his wife, and then said to me, "Can we send you guys tickets for early June?" He asked me if I had any questions.

I did. I wanted to ask, casually, "Do you think the huge, fat larval flying things in my kitchen are termites?" I dug my fingernails into my hairline to calm myself, like a teen-age cutter without the courage of her convictions.

I do not know *why* I thought it made sense to go, in my condition at the time. My friend Tom says that "Why?" is not a useful question.

The question I asked myself was: "How bad could one trip be?" This is what I would like on my tombstone. The answer this time was: From the first morning after they picked us up at the airport until the last, miserable morning, it felt like junior high. With the strain of feeling like the country cousin, the poor relation, I felt as if I were having a nervous breakdown. I felt jealous, alone, defensive. Everything the couple said about the new house, the impending movie deal, and their marriage set me on edge. I flinched, cringed, skulked, and lied in my good-girl voice. I hid in my room, weeping, and rang up a $400 phone bill talking to my therapist in California.

I'm not going to excuse my behavior with examples of what they said that triggered me. Well, maybe just one:

Some friends of theirs came out for a picnic on the beach at sunset, a handsome couple with adorable children. It was the third day, and I had already started to go bad, like a soft cheese.

My hostess had had intestinal distress all day and could manage only saltines and ginger ale on the beach. So I ate for two, out of general unhappiness. When Sam insolently tossed his sandwich into the sand, I overreacted, grabbed his arm too tightly, and made him cry. The other children huddled with their parents. I rushed to apologize and comfort Sam, but it was too late. Everyone could see who I was — the

Bad Seed in the sequel, *Motherhood*. And then, as if I were an eight-year-old, I was sent to my room.

My host suggested firmly that I go inside and collect myself.

And the most stunning part of the story is that I did.

I went to my room, on the second floor, and left a message for my therapist, who was not in. I stared out the window, the girl who used to gaze miserably down at the ground from her dentist's fourteenth-floor office in San Francisco, wanting to jump. One of my earliest memories is going with my mother and older brother into San Francisco on the Greyhound to see our dentist. I wear a camel's-hair coat and short white gloves; my brother wears slacks and a clip-on bow tie. If we are both good, we will go to Blum's for coffee crunch cake when we are done. I am alone in the dentist's waiting room, drawn as if by a magnet to the window, seeing myself unlock the window and climb out, seeing myself fall onto the pedestrians on Sutter. Instead I run to the coffee table and hurl myself into *Highlights for Children*, lost and terrified, searching the full-page drawing of a tree for all fifteen objects hidden within, a toucan, a bicycle, a shoe.

When my therapist called back, she reminded me that my hosts were not the problem: if you've got a problem, you usually have to go look in the mirror. They had been caught up in my childhood drama; they were in my life to help me heal something old. She had me get myself a cup of tea and wrap myself in a shawl. My mental fever broke. I made a fire in the fireplace downstairs. When everyone trooped in from the beach, Sam came over to cuddle with me, and I hung my head and made an apology to everyone. The couple and their guests were kind and understanding. We sat by the fire, warming ourselves. Then my hostess, holding her stomach and laughing prettily, said, "I just don't think I have *ever* felt so thin and so rich."

We all laughed — what a witty thing to say! After a while, we all went to bed, and first thing in the morning, I sneaked into town, found a pay phone, and changed our return reservation to the next day.

When I told the couple this later in the day, they were angry: I was wrecking the vacation, I was being secretive and controlling — which was and is true, and which probably ever more shall be.

Sam and I left the next day, and I have not seen the couple since.

We spoke about two weeks later. They were still upset about my behavior. I apologized and said I'd try to make amends, as soon as I could.

It has taken me only twelve years.

I don't know why all of a sudden I began to feel haunted by the experience, the ruined friendship, this one particular garbage heap. But I kept getting the Holy Spirit nudge, and the other day I sat down and wrote them a letter, and tried to clean up my mess.

I said that I hated what had happened, and my part in it, and that it had made my heart ache over the years. I did not explain or justify my triggers — the jealousy, especially, because trigger implies weapons, weapons imply aim, aim implies combat, combat implies engagement. All I wanted was to feel *less* engaged, less stuck: I wanted to let it go, which is *so* not my strong suit, any more than forgiveness is. I wanted to be a person of peace, who diminishes hurt in the world, instead of perpetrating it.

But I felt scared. Will they write back, and what will they write, and what if they don't? What if they're reading my letter out loud and snickering, or reading it to their friends from the picnic, and they're all comparing notes on how crazy I am? Maybe they forgive me, maybe they don't. But I finally, finally forgive me; sort of–ish. No curtain of light or soft angel voices, but the understanding that forgiving myself makes it possible to forgive them, too. Maybe this is grace, or simply the passage of time. Whatever you want to call this, I'll take it. I paid through the nose for this one.

All I know is, I was able to pick up a pen. I said it, I sent it, and the best I could do, surprisingly, seems to be enough. As of this writing, months later, they have not written back, but I'm no longer crouched over the problem, looking furtively over my shoulder. I'm lurching forward in my life again, and it feels as if someone finally cracked open a window that had been jammed.

THE CARPET GUY

I was driving along one day not too long ago when I passed a small carpet store nestled between several taller commercial buildings. It had been sandwiched there forever; you'd expect to find it gone some-day, like a missing tooth. In front was the perfect carpet remnant for our children's room at church, rolled up and leaning against a fence. It was sea-foam green, and only fifty dollars. I pulled over, picked up the rug, walked into the store, and gave the man behind the desk fifty dollars in cash.

"This is perfect for our nursery school at church," I enthused. He was middle-aged, plain, and so quiet that at first I thought he might be mute. He gave me a receipt, and we said good-bye.

That Sunday, I dropped the rolled-up carpet in the room where the little kids meet. One of the mothers called me the next day. She said that when they had unrolled the carpet, they found a moldy spot in the middle, and so she returned it to the carpet guy.

"Did you get our money back?"

"No, his bookkeeper wasn't there. But he'll have the money later today. Can you pick it up? And bring your receipt."

I stopped by the store the following day. "Hi," I said to the man. "I'm from the church. We had to return a rug, and the woman who dropped it off said you would reimburse me."

There was a moment's pause. "Someone already picked up the money."

"That's not possible," I explained. "No one else would have picked it up."

I fished my receipt from my purse, and held it out to him. He studied it, nodded. "Someone picked up the money. An hour ago."

"But no one else would have picked it up."

We both held out our palms, the universal sign of being amiably perplexed.

I was not particularly alarmed at this point. There had been a simple misunderstanding, I felt, and we could clear it up. If you are sincere and rational, and trust in goodness enough, everything sorts itself out.

I went to a pay phone and called the woman who had returned the rug. "Did you stop by and pick up the money from the carpet guy?" I asked.

"No, I thought you were going to."

I went back to the store. The man was finishing up some business with another customer, so I waited. This time I noticed how crummy the place was. Carpets were rolled up by the dozens, stacked to the ceiling like timber, and the lights were dim; this was a place where something bad was going down, it seemed.

When the other customer left, I threw my hands up with a faint maternal gesture of displeasure. "No one else picked up the money," I said.

"Yes," the man answered. "An hour ago." He tapped his ledger; it was soiled, and filled with tiny words and numbers. A pencil notation in the margin read *$50.00*. He tapped it. "Fifty dollars."

"Look," I said, now in my sternest Sunday-school-teacher voice. "I don't want to make trouble. But no one picked up the money. And I'd like it. Now."

He tapped the *$50.00* again.

"That doesn't mean anything," I said. "I'm from a *Sunday* school. This is for little children." For good measure I added, "With *asthma*."

He tapped the ledger yet again, then

138

waved me away, like a servant, or a bee. This wasn't fair! I wanted to wail, wounded and self-righteous.

"Hey," I said. *"Buddy."* I had my hands on my hips, and I glared. I was as furious as I can ever remember being, thinking about the innocent little children at our Sunday school, the asthmatic little children, scampering about on the mold, seizing up. Sunday school made me remember to pray — Help! Help!

I got my answer: Start behaving well, and you will feel better. This is what Jesus would want, and he had to be there in the rug store. Maybe he was being embarrassed to tears, like when your kid has a tantrum in public. I stared off at the log-pile of rugs. I was trembling; you could have cracked walnuts with my self-righteousness. Jesus doesn't hold this against a person. His message is that we're all sort of nuts and suspicious and petty and full of crazy hungers, and everything feels awful a lot of the time, but even so — one's behavior needs to be better. One needs to be decent. So I would try.

"We've got a problem," I said.

He rolled his eyes. See — that's where decency will get you, I thought. I tried another tack: "Do you want me to call the police? Huh? How about that?"

He waved me away again. The door to the most primitive place inside me opened, where the betrayed child lives, terrified, wounded, murderous. On top of everything, I felt a deep, familiar self-loathing.

As we glared at each other, I found it kind of heady, like a drug. But I stormed home and called a man who went to my church, Sam's Big Brother, Brian. Although he is not formally a member of Big Brothers, he has been helping me raise Sam since before he was born; he's Sam's forty-five-year-old brother. He does not look the part of an enforcer — he is owlish and sturdy and enthusiastically neutral, positive and well behaved. Not at all a hired-assassin type. However, he was coming by to see Sam that night. So there was that.

I told him the whole story over the phone.

He was flabbergasted. "How about if I call him?" he volunteered. "And I'll call you right back."

He didn't call for half an hour, and when he did, he had been reduced to the same contagious craziness I had been in. "I told him I hoped I wouldn't have to come down there after work. But he hung up on me twice."

"So how did you leave it?"

140

"I said I'm stopping by after work today, at five. And he better have it."

I went for a walk: that is what Jesus always did. He gave crazy people some space. He would say, "Go ahead. You're a mess. Go be a mess. Work it out. We'll talk again."

I was still a mess when Brian arrived at our house at five-thirty.

"God, I wanted to kill the guy!" he reported. "He kept saying someone else had picked up the money and pointing to his ledger."

"Did you get the money?"

"No — but he promised he'll have it tomorrow. His bookkeeper wasn't there."

I put my head in my hands. First the man had said someone had already picked it up. Now we were back to pretending he had a bookkeeper.

The next morning I stopped by the rug store again. I had said my prayers. I had asked to be respectful and not lose my mind. A balding man with a long ponytail was sitting with the carpet guy at his desk, both of them smoking.

"Hi," I said, nicely, to the carpet guy. "My friend Brian said you would have the money if I stopped by today."

He looked at me and smirked. Then he turned to his friend and twirled his finger near his ear, the universal sign for loco. This cracked his friend up.

I fumed, twisting in the wind. "Where the fuck is my money?" I demanded.

"It has been taken care of," the man told his friend, who nodded.

And I fell right past my fixation with being right, into the dark, swampy underside of human discourse. I found a weird nourishment in our exchange. I was very focused. I saw myself choking the man with my bare hands, but instead, desperate, I grabbed his phone off the desk. And in the most menacing way possible, I started dialing.

I called Brian at his office, while brandishing the phone like a grenade.

"He won't give me the money," I told Brian, not taking my eyes off the man.

"Put him on the line," said Brian.

I handed the man the phone. He held it to his ear. Then I heard a voice from the other end that sounded like Tony Soprano. But it was dear churchgoing Brian, saying, "Don't make me come down there again! You are doomed if I have to come down there again! Give her the goddamn money!"

The man shook his head and sneered. "Fifty dollars," he said ruefully, like, I wouldn't normally put up with this shit unless it was *way* more than fifty dollars. He opened his top drawer and took out a checkbook. "Fifty dollars," he said in a comical voice, as if he were horsing around for a child as he wrote.

He wrote a check for fifty dollars, leaving the "Pay to the order of" blank, handed it to me.

"Thank you," I said grimly.

I headed for the bank, which is a couple of blocks away. I filled in my name, endorsed the check, and handed it to the teller. A moment later, she said, "Oh. I'm sorry. There are insufficient funds."

I finally laughed, into my chest, quietly. "It's okay," I said. I took the check and turned away. If you had seen me, you'd have thought she had just given me a hundred dollars for being so nice about the whole thing.

I sat outside the bank for a while. Look, I said to God, it's to You, pal. You copy that? Then I sat in the sun and kept starting to laugh. I felt deep inside that I'd gotten it, though I could not quite have said *what* I'd gotten. I didn't get the delicious taste of release I'd been expecting, when a wrong has been righted, but I got something better, a kind of miracle: I stopped hating myself. The carpet guy had cheated me, but he was also an innocent bystander in a very old story: he was the ledger inside me of every time I'd been humiliated and stiffed.

Well, I said to God, the Eagle has landed. Now what am I supposed to do? After a few minutes, I knew: I got the noodge in my heart to go to the Safeway near the rug store and buy a bouquet of daisies for the carpet man. One has a moral and a spiritual obligation to clean up one's side of the street. I wrote him a note: "Here is your check back. I am very sorry for the way I behaved. Anne."

The carpet store was locked, but the dim lights were on. I knocked softly. When no one opened the door, I tied the daisies to the doorknob with the metal twist-tie that held them, and dropped the check and my note through the mail slot. Maybe this was what Ecclesiastes meant about casting your bread upon the water; it's so little, usually only crumbs, but how nourishing the casting is.

And then I went back home.

I called the carpet store from my kitchen at five, for no reason. I recognized the man's voice when he answered.

"Hi," I said. "This is Anne Lamott." There was a silence, loud and dark.

"I got your letter," he said. "That was a decent thing." And just as I began to savor his words, he added, "But you behaved badly!"

I had behaved badly? It all started up in me again, but this time it didn't take over, because something got there first. You want to know how big God's love is? The answer is: It's very big. It's bigger than you're comfortable with.

"Yes, I know," I said. It was true and it was all confusing.

We're invited more deeply into this mystery on a daily basis, to be here as one-of; a mess like everyone else, and not in charge. That's why we hate it.

There was another silence, and then we said good night at almost the same time.

DANDELIONS

I don't hate anyone right now, not even George W. Bush. This may seem an impossibility, but it is true, and indicates the presence of grace, or dementia, or both. While I still oppose every decision he makes and am appalled at his general level of malfunction, I no longer want to hurt him. I'd like to see him be run out of office, but as I've been making friends with the hatred and cruelty in me, my heart has softened slightly, as if treated with a meat tenderizer. Not hating Bush has brought with it several astonishing gifts. One is that the less I am consumed by him, the more I can be consumed by, well, myself, and those things I love about life. I seem to hang on to my hates because they help take my mind off the cracked reflection in the mirror. Another gift is that I can model genuine forgiveness toward Sam, and demonstrate that in this cold, scary world, whenever possible, we pick up after ourselves and turn up the flame of our lanterns just a smidge. Learning to unhate Bush has also given me the tools to learn to forgive several other people, including most recently the husband of one of my best friends.

Nell's husband has short-man syndrome. Eddie is one of those deadly dull people who is so upbeat that I suspect he would subconsciously like to go through the neighborhood, house by house, with a machine gun. He seems oblivious of the effect that his long, rambling monologues have on people — he doesn't notice the blank faces, the fingers flexing like those of people buried alive, the ocular tics. You could write down his words verbatim, show them to him, and he'd probably say, "I know someone just like that!" Then he'd tell you about that person until your teeth hurt. His hostage-taking is passive-aggressive, and is only one reason I dislike him. A good marriage is supposed to be one where each spouse secretly thinks he or she got the better deal; but Eddie — and this is another reason I dislike him — thinks Nell got the better deal, because she got him: he married her even though she was heavy. She's a nearly perfect human being, while he talks too much, desperate for love and, on top of it all, arrogant. In other words, except for his dullness, he and I have a lot in common.

The polite answer to why Nell married him is: Nell *settled.* This happens with one's coolest girlfriends, who sometimes mate with people not worthy to drink their bathwater, and I mean that in a warm and nonjudgmental way.

I learned how to unhate Bush the only way people ever really learn things — by doing. It's a terrible system. If I were God, I would have provided a much easier way — an Idiot's Guide, or a spiritual ATM, or maybe some kind of compromise. But no, even the second person of the Trinity had to learn by doing, by failing, by feeling, by being amazed. God sent Jesus to join the human experience, which means to make a lot of mistakes. Jesus didn't arrive here knowing how to walk. He had fingers and toes, confusion, sexual feelings, crazy human internal processes. He had the same prejudices as the rest of his tribe: he had to learn that the Canaanite woman was a person. He had to suffer the hardships and tedium and setbacks of being a regular person. If he hadn't, the Incarnation would mean nothing.

When it came to Bush, I had to pull out

all the stops. Big sickness, big medicine: I talked to spiritual people with a black sense of humor, read great works on forgiveness, and repeatedly prayed that I would not hate him. Somehow this torrent flushed some of the gunk out of the dirty cup of me. I forced myself to turn off CNN and to put aside more time to sit in stillness. And I realized once again that we're punished not for our hatred, for not forgiving people, but *by* it. Miraculously, I finally got sick and tired of feeling punished by Bush. I drank more water, which moves things. All of this jiggled some plaque off me like an electric toothbrush in super slo-mo. (And to be honest, it helped beyond words when Bush's approval ratings began to tank. More than anything.)

With Eddie, there has never been real incentive to learn to love him, because I disliked him only a little. Bush was my highwater mark. Eddie did not make me recoil, but before Nell was diagnosed with cancer, I avoided him because he would be so longwinded and upbeat. Sometimes when I went over to pick her up for the movies, he'd trap me in the doorway like a bouncer at a bar. All of Nell's friends gossiped about him, because he was so aggressively boring. Worst of all, he made little digs about Nell's weight and absentmindedness, as if we would ever collude with him. She mentioned smirky things he had said to her over time that girlfriends simply can't forgive. But after Nell got sick, I was relieved that she had Eddie to help her through chemo, and to sleep with, even though she did not love or even really like him. Now that Nell was almost done with treatment, however, I was sad that she'd never be able to get rid of him, with all he was doing for her. No more "Give Eddie enough rope" years. They had not been lovers in years. They were roommates.

One morning recently, after I dropped off some soup for Nell at their house, Eddie tried to trap me with his butterfly net. I race-walked to my car, pretending not to hear him calling me, and realized immediately that I was being an asshole. This was ridiculous — it was only hurting me. Maybe the hate in me that comes with the human package was looking for a place to roost.

Last week, I was given a chance to learn to love, or at least like, Eddie.

It started off poorly, as these things usually do, and without my approval. Our county was having a rare late-spring heat wave, and by ten a.m. I was already pinned to the couch. Sweat pooled underneath me.

The heat had stolen the glossy briskness of my everyday life, and I was about to take a nap when Nell called and badgered me into taking a walk with her.

We met at the trailhead. She used to have long, thick blond hair and boundless energy; now she is bald and moves like an old woman with gout. She is still beautiful, even stripped of so much, but pretty like a girl playing dress-up, with her scarf and light pink lipstick, her mother-of-pearl earrings. I love it. We started up the trail, breathing in the fresh, grassy, laundry smells. The geodesic dandelions next to the dirt road looked like disco balls. If you were making a movie on a really low budget, you could use them as your space station, but after you make a wish and blow away the white fluff, they resemble any old dandelions.

Nell looked at me unhappily. I asked her what was wrong, fearing it was bad cancer news, but she dismissed the very suggestion. "Oh God, no," she said, "I am like *totally* sort of whatever about that," which is a very Nell thing to say. Also, if you think about it, it's a profound spiritual stance, to be totally sort of whatever about something this scary. The trouble, she told me, was that during her last, miserable stretch in bed, Eddie had bought a central air conditioner, on sale, marked down from $4,000 to $2,500, with the money they'd been saving for vacation.

"Why did he do that?" I asked.

"It was a great deal," she said. "And he was hot."

The sun blazed down on us. I took it personally, as I do everything — I can't seem to learn how *not* to, or at any rate, I'm the slowest learner in class. I used to be one of the quickest. My teachers read special texts with me in the back of our classrooms while the other kids worked their lessons. I thought of Henry Tanner's famous painting of Christ learning to read. Jesus is a boy of seven or eight, standing beside Mary, touching the words on a scroll, figuring out each word as he goes. He had to learn to read from scratch, with the alphabet, the way I did. He did not have infused knowledge: he was born not knowing anything. And hey, *I* was only *four* when I taught myself to read. Maybe Jesus struggled with reading. I'm just saying. So, after all, maybe there was hope for me in areas where I'd been behind.

Nell continued talking. Their house got plenty of shade and had fans in every room. And freon is so bad for the environment. Plus, she'd so wanted a vacation when she was done with chemo. But Eddie had spent that money.

"Can't he return it?"

"It was a floor sample. Final sale."

What an idiot, I thought, even as, walking along feeling weak and exhausted from the heat, I understood why he'd done it. I wanted air, too, and believed that if I had it, my house would be perfect. I'll go to my grave convinced that you can find happiness out there, somewhere, with the right someone or good financing. If you could just get things to line up properly, you could relax, learn to experience life in all its immediacy, reconnect with who you really are, with the soul or spirit, the divine whatchacallit deep inside that sparks when it hears certain music.

We're not stupid, Eddie and I. We are Americans.

"And it's broken," Nell said mournfully, "sitting in our driveway, waiting for the Sears repair guy. He's supposed to come today."

I smiled, remembering all the friendly repair guys in their Sears uniforms who came to our house to fix things when I was young. My mother loved them, the way I love my pastor. She fussed over them and fed them homemade brownies. This triggered my memory of all the men like Eddie whom my mother hated, all the reasonably good-looking men in town who thought they were so charming, who were not good enough for their wives, and who then left them during the diaspora of the early sixties. My mother had incredible women friends, many of them married to ridiculous, arrogant men. There were also men whose wives came to our house in the middle of the night with bruises. "What a son of a bitch," my mother would say of any man who left his wife to marry a younger woman, who stayed but was not faithful, who remained young and trim while his wife got fat, or any man whom she'd voted for who shipped American boys to Vietnam. "He got what he deserved," she'd pronounce if someone lost his job or had a heart attack or, in one special case, an amputation. "He was a son of a bitch." It was a black-and-white world, like Bush's or any fundamentalist's. She distrusted most handsome men, because my father did not love her and was handsome. "So-and-so *is* handsome, but he's a son of a bitch, like all those Kennedys." Yet she *loved* the Kennedys, and cried for years about Bobby's death.

So I grew up a little confused.

I thought about the air conditioner for a moment. "Maybe this is happening for a reason," I volunteered. "Our lives are *filled* with people who provoke us, especially people we love. They help us figure out our own shit and why we are here."

"And why are we here again?"

I shrugged. "We don't know." Nell smiled. "We only sort of know," I said. "To live, love, help — to decorate. To sweep our huts and find some food."

Turkey vultures circled above. Speaking of which.

"Let's turn around," she said. "I'm beat."

I could see that she was not only tired, but sick as well. How had I not noticed her terrible color, her skin pale and flushed at the same time? Her cheekbones stuck out like bad implants. My highest self, my conscience, whatever it was, grabbed me by the shoulders and said: "You are such an asshole! You see her every few days, but Eddie sees her at her worst, after chemo, sick, tired, asleep. God! Get that container of Accent out."

I imagined Eddie, in the driveway with the Sears guy, trying to stave off death with an air conditioner — it reminded me of Sam when he was little, asking me what we would do if a man came into our house at night with a machine gun. When I shrugged, he ran around the house, gathering tennis rackets, bricks, steak knives, and a fire poker, and then stashed them under my bed.

I took Nell's hand and started to cry, out of general misery for all of us — for Nell, for me and my angry delusions, for Sam with only me to protect him, for Eddie watching Nell sleep beside him. I opened my eyes wide the way I did as a child, to spread the tears so they wouldn't pool and fall. When my nose started to run, I wiped it on the top of my T-shirt. Nell looked over at me and stuck out her lower lip. She rubbed my arms briskly. "Look," she said. "I'm okay now, and you're okay. Right? That's a lot. And either they'll get it running or it'll make a great planter."

We stopped to drink from our water bottles. The vegetation was unusually dense this year, after the rainiest winter of our lives. It was as green as hills in Ireland. The grass would turn dry and golden soon, after the earliest heat wave any of us could remember. In the old days, I would have blamed both the rain and the heat on Bush — his lethal environmental policies and all that goddamn brush-clearing. Now I looked around at the wild flowers and grasses. Wild irises were still growing — unheard of in late May. People had even seen mountain lions this year, although bobcats were much more common, standing on hillocks watching you approach, like gatekeepers. There were also deer and baby rabbits, everywhere.

"It's sort of sweet," I said, "that Eddie spent *his* vacation money, too. He wanted to show you he's there for you, and your house will be so cool."

"It will," she said. "Eat your heart out."

Me? I was planning to go home and crawl into bed. When it's so hot, you need to take off even your lightest blanket and lie between the sheets. You can make a cave with the top sheet, make your own world inside a cotton tent, where there's shade, and you can be your sweaty animal self and no one else can get in. There were fields like that where we were walking, hidden from the beaten paths on these hillsides, where you could step out of the heat into a glade, and there are huge tufts of coarse deer fur that they've shed all over the grasses and coyote bush, so it looks like it's been snowing.

NEAR THE LAGOON, 2004

It is autumn now, following a treacherous August, and I awoke this morning to find that the leaves in my heart have started changing color, from green to yellow, persimmon, and red.

After a rainy morning yesterday, both sun and clouds were out when several friends and I headed through the West Marin corridor, past meadows full of cows and horses, and hills of dry, lion-colored grass. We drove through the small rural and hippie towns on the way to the ocean, out to Bolinas, where I lived when I was in my twenties. I was an out-of-control alcoholic then — but in a good way, I had thought. A festive way. Along with the beverages, I took a lot of drugs, which sometimes expanded my mind, but other times caused me accidentally to sleep with other women's husbands. I hurt some innocent people along the way. I also began my life as a writer there, describing the mountains, the beaches, the tide pools, the lagoon, the pelicans, the ocean, the marvelous life and values of the community. But when I was in my mid-twenties, the world came to an end: my father died in our family's cabin above Duxbury Reef, half an hour's walk from the Bolinas lagoon, where we went birding every week. It only took ten to fifteen years to bounce back from that.

We were headed to that lagoon yesterday, and that is very rare for me, as I have stayed out of the town for most of the twenty-two years since I left. It is too painful to go there; it's filled with the huge, gaping absence of my father, and with the faces of people who loved me, or didn't, whom I hurt so egregiously, or by whom I was hurt or abandoned. But I still have a couple of friends there. One of them, Megan, is a cofounder of the Mainstreet Moms: Organize or Bust (themmob.org), which has grown from a ragtag group of a few mothers into a thriving grassroots organization helping women (especially mothers) in swing states register to vote. Members send packets to volunteers across the country, with names and addresses of unregistered women voters, pretty stationery, decorative stickers, and sample letters. The volunteers write to the women, who thought they didn't count, and tell them that they do.

The group was having a fund-raiser, a picnic by the lagoon, and I was going to do a reading. I didn't remember walking to the lagoon in the years since I'd left, until my friends and I headed down a private path that led from the town's main road.

I almost immediately got a Twilight Zone feeling. First, I was going back to the place from which I had fled, and that is usually a signal to me that something mythical is in the works. And second, instantly a hobgoblin of a man appeared in our path, in overalls, with chin hairs and a pointy hat — the whole gestalt. He asked, with raised eyebrows and a portentous tone, "Do you know where you are going?"

We didn't. He described a meandering path to the water.

Next we came upon some tall, thin wood posts, like stripped tree trunks, very Native American, with a hint of maypole, festooned with yellow silk streamers. We looked up to find a horde of children ahead, swinging on tire swings tied to tree branches, playing on hay bales, all of them in bright colors, wearing tie-dye, overalls, sequins.

It was like an updated scene from Brueghel, with that amazing shifting light. There were those hay bales, and then people in farming clothes and hippie peasant wear, none of the black you see in cities, but instead the colors of flowers and Necco wafers. There were tables covered with exquisite natural foods, raised and produced locally, none of that weird seitan and mochi that make you feel like an abused astronaut, but barbecued oysters and sausages, cornucopias of bright salad, and pastry. A few hundred people sat eating under the trees and in the sun. Tables were set up where you could make or buy beaded necklaces with clay letter charms spelling out "Vote." It was like a hippie fair, with a single theme: Vote. And there were tables covered with voter packets that you could take home, with their lists of names and addresses of unregistered women voters, lavender paper, aqua envelopes, silver stars. Sweet hippie musicians were playing protest songs, not with the heavy-metal polemics or rap you might hear at some antiwar rallies, but herbal-essence guitar and harp polemics about peace and love and freedom. They led us in singing "America the Beautiful," and I felt dizzy with joy in the patriotism and connection, glad to be amid all this good, loving, angry, dissident energy, which can still — *still* — happen in this country.

You can't always live in furious emergency, and for all that mess and defeat and grief Democrats had been feeling over the 2000 presidential election to be transformed into beauty and work, well — this was brilliant, and brave.

The town and the townspeople had grown up since I'd been away. I checked in with a number of the grown-up kids I'd been closest to when I was in my twenties, as if they were on a birding list at Audubon Canyon Ranch. They had been elementary school-aged then, or teenagers. I had driven them around town once when I was on acid. I had slept with some of their fathers. But they had adored me, because I was a good listener, funny, and halfway between their parents' ages and their own. I thank God that they survived loving me. Many of them now had kids of their own, who were on the tire swings we had passed. Their parents were grandparents, or ersatz grandparents, broader in the beam and going gray. The former kids were in their thirties now, and a number of them appeared to be drinking a lot or drug-addicted. This can be a tough town.

The light on the lagoon and the field shifted constantly, bright in contrast to the glower of the morning. The tide was so high that it looked as if the lagoon could have leapt over the meadow into the clearing where we had gathered.

At the same time I felt that happiness, seeing these old friends, I kept saying to my companions, God, I hope so-and-so isn't here — and then that person would suddenly appear. Sometimes it was an old lover, or one of the women I had betrayed, or someone I had dropped or been dropped by. I had tried to clean things up efficiently when I got sober, but with wounds to the heart, the healing is expensive and circuitous.

Still, in each case, everyone wanted to hug and kiss me; eventually.

The morning rain had left a sprinkly shine on the leaves.

It had been twenty-two calendar years since I'd moved, but my relationship to this town and these people has always taken place outside time. Maybe it was all those drugs, or the suspended animation of my father's long illness, but I don't think so. It feels more like the way soul time passes, like when your baby turns one week old, or when you're with someone who will probably die that day. But now I was with all these people, some of them firebrand activists but most of them regular old people, and it felt quite natural. We had gone beyond an absurd and terrible time in our lives, the first four years of George W. Bush's presidency; then tapped into ordinariness, and let it guide us to this gathering. That is what happens in fairy tales: the wound or the danger guides you straight into the heart of itself, and you end up finding you.

I found some of that yesterday by the lagoon, that mysterious shy familiarity with a community that had helped form me. I was there because nine months before, some people had gotten to such a level of fear and frustration with the government that, instead of stomping off and saying, "This is so fucked, and so hopeless," they had decided to register as many mothers as they could in swing states, by writing to them. And they invited me to help raise money for their effort.

The first month, they sent out five thousand letters. By Election Day 2004, they had sent out 201,000 — five thousand alone on the day before the fund-raiser.

Some people might think that writing letters to unregistered women voters is a pathetic howling in the wind, totally self-serving, like being willing to face people from a sometimes messy past and trying to make amends. This is how the pendulum shifts slowly in the other direction, by the very act of howling in the wind, which always blows back eventually, a breeze carrying seeds.

People seemed to love my reading, which lasted half an hour; I realized that I will always be family to the people of this town. It got cold not long after I finished. The clouds that had threatened rain were breaking up, but kept hanging there in front of the sun, like memories. On top of everything, I felt grief and a deep, scary discomfort. In a fairy tale, you often have to leave the place where you have grown comfortable and travel to a fearful place full of pain, and search for what was stolen or confront the occupying villain; it takes time for the resulting changes to integrate themselves into the small, funky moments that make up our lives. All that mess I had made, all that love and damage, all those connections, those ghosts and those children who were parents to the children on the swings — all of this was part of the lava lamp inside me, inside my life. It was like finding a long-lost heirloom. Thirty-five years ago, at the Fillmore in San Francisco, or more recently at peace marches, the energy would sometimes pull in a direction you wanted to go, where what you were doing was real, and counted:

it was going to work. Then, all of a sudden, people would pass a balloon around overhead, and everyone would tap it as it floated by, lifting all that energy with the lightest touch.

■ ■ ■ ■

Lost and Found

■ ■ ■ ■

If I don't have red, I use blue.
— Pablo Picasso

STEINBECK COUNTRY

In Salinas, word went out. This is how many tribal stories begin: word goes out to the people of a community that there is a great danger or that a wrong is being committed. This is how I first found out that the governor planned to close the public libraries in Salinas, making it the largest city in the United States to lose its libraries because of budget cuts.

Without getting into any mudslinging about whether or not our leaders are clueless, bullying, nonreading numbskulls, let me just say that when word went out that the three libraries — the John Steinbeck, the Cesar Chavez, and El Gabilan — were scheduled for closing, a whole lot of people rose up as one to say, This does not work for us.

Salinas is one of the poorest communities in the state of California, in one of the richest counties in the country. The city and the surrounding area serve as the setting for so many of Steinbeck's great novels. Think farmworkers, fields of artichokes and garlic, faded stucco houses stained with dirt, tracts of ticky-tacky housing, James Dean's face in *East of Eden,* strawberry fields, and old gas stations.

Now think about closing the libraries there, closing the buildings that hold the town's books, all those stories about people and wisdom and justice and life and silliness and laborers bending low to pick the strawberries. You'd have to be crazy to bring such obvious karmic repercussions down on yourself. So in early April, a group of writers and actors fought back, showing up in Salinas for a twenty-four-hour "emergency read-in."

My sad sixties heart soared like an eagle at contemplating the very name: *emergency read-in.* George W. Bush and John Ashcroft had tried for years to create a country the East German state could only dream about, empowering the government to keep track of the books we checked out or bought, all in the name of national security. But the president and the attorney general hadn't counted on how passionately writers and readers feel about the world, or at any rate, the worlds contained inside the silent spines of books.

We came together because we started out as children who were saved by stories, stories read to us at night when we were little, stories we read by ourselves, in which we could get lost and thereby found. Some of us had grown up to become people with loud voices, which the farmworkers and their children needed. And we were mad. Show a bunch of writers a sealed library, and they see red. Perhaps we were a little sensitive or overwrought, but in this case we saw a one-way tunnel into the dark. We saw the beginnings of fascism.

A free public library is a revolutionary notion, and when people don't have free access to books, then communities are like radios without batteries. You cut people off from essential sources of information — mythical, practical, linguistic, political — and you break them. You render them helpless in the face of political oppression. We were not going to let this happen.

Writers and actors came from San Francisco and San Jose, from all around. Maxine Hong Kingston came from Oakland. Hector Elizondo drove up from Los Angeles, as did Mike Farrell. The poet José Montoya drove from Sacramento, four hours away. Alisa Valdes-Rodriguez flew all morn-

171

ing to be there. I drove down from the Bay area with the Buddhist writer and teacher Jack Kornfield.

When we arrived, the lawn outside the Chavez library held only about 150 people — not the throngs we had hoped for — but the community was especially welcoming and grateful, and the women of CodePink, who helped organize the event, kept everyone's spirits up. It's hard to be depressed when activists in pink feather boas are kissing you. Many people had pitched tents on one side of the library, where they could rest through the night while the readings were proceeding onstage.

Can you imagine the kind of person who is willing to stay up all night in the cold to keep a few condemned libraries open?

Well, not me, baby.

I was going home to my own bed that night. But then I saw some of my parents' old friends who were planning to stay, people who have been protesting and rallying in civil rights and peace marches since I was a girl, people who had driven from San Francisco because they've always known that the only thing that keeps a democracy functioning is the constant education of its citizens. If you don't have a place where the poor, the marginalized, and the young can find out who they are, then you have no hope of maintaining a free and civilized society.

We were there to celebrate some of the rare intelligence capabilities that our country can actually be proud of — those of librarians. I see them as healers and magicians. Librarians can tease out of inarticulate individuals enough information about what they are after to lead them on the path of connection. They are trail guides through the forest of shelves and aisles — you turn a person loose who has limited skills, and he'll be walloped by the branches. But librarians match up readers with the right books: "Hey, is this one too complicated? Then why don't you give this one a try?"

Inside the library were Hispanic children and teenagers and their parents, and a few old souls. They sat in chairs reading, stood surveying the bilingual collection, and worked at the computers. These computers are the only ones that a lot of people in town have access to. The after-school literacy and homework programs at the libraries are among the few safe places where parents can direct their children, away from the gangs.

On this afternoon, parents read to their children in whispered Spanish, and the air

173

felt nutritious. As Barry Lopez once said, "Sometimes a person needs a story more than food to stay alive."

I went back outside. Poets of every color were reading. People milled around with antiwar placards — *"¡Libros sí! ¡Bombas no!"* Older members of the community told stories from legends, history, their own families. Fernando Suarez stepped up to the mike and spoke of his nineteen-year-old son, who had died not long before in Iraq. Suarez spoke first in English and then in Spanish, as he does frequently around the country, and your heart could hardly beat for the sadness.

Maybe in Oaxaca children are still hearing the stories that the elders tell, but these kids in Salinas are being raised by television sets: they are latchkey kids. Their parents work for the most part in the fields and in wealthy homes. If you are mesmerized by televised stupidity, and don't get to hear or read stories about your world, you can be fooled into thinking that the world isn't miraculous — and it is.

The media attention brought in enough money, partly as a result of that day, to keep the libraries open for a whole year. You might not call this a miracle, exactly, but if you had been at the emergency read-in, you would see that it was at least the beginning of one.

A bunch of normally self-obsessed artist types came together to say to the people of Salinas: We care about your children, your stories, and your freedom. Something has gone so wrong in this country that needs to be fixed, and we care about that. Reading and books are medicine. Stories are written and told by and for people who have been broken, but who have risen up, or will rise, if attention is paid to them. Those people are you and us. Stories and truth are splints for the soul, and that makes today a sacred gathering. Now we were all saying: Pass it on.

SHADOWS

Late one night I got into a cab at the San Francisco airport and headed home after two nights of travel. I was tired and rattled after a turbulent flight, so I was grateful that the organizers of the conference where I'd just spoken had arranged for a car to pick me up and take me home. The driver was waiting for me in the baggage area, wearing a black suit and tie, holding a sign with my name on it. He was very handsome, like Marlon Brando, and must have weighed close to four hundred pounds.

I had spoken that day on spirituality, and therefore felt evolved enough to know his body and biography were not who he was: that his soul, the glow of the eternal divine deep inside him, was the truth of his identity. People stared at him as we walked through the airport to the parking lot; I walked tall and protectively beside him. It goes without saying that many people see fatness as a moral matter that everyone can agree on — they believe that even Jesus was deeply offended. That he hated heavy people, but those parts had to be taken out of the Gospels because they were so cruel.

In the car, Mozart was on the radio, a clarinet concerto so piercingly beautiful that something inside me woke up with a myclonic jerk, like someone revived with smelling salts or waking abruptly after dozing off at the movies. I closed my eyes to listen.

When the piece ended and I opened my eyes, we were driving past the graveyards of Colma, ten minutes from the airport, where naturally a girl's thoughts turn to how many veterans are buried there, and how she feels about chickenhawk leadership. I was used to this: I had been angry all summer, let alone the last few years, as things in Iraq continued to deteriorate, and this anger, combined with a month of intensely hot weather, had left my soul feeling deeply worn-out. The one thing that revived it was to clean my house. Puttering helped, as did sweeping and working with my hands at simple tasks like washing dishes, because it's monk work.

The driver pointed out all the crosses. I nodded.

"I have cosmic contact with this place,"

he said, "even though I didn't see it for the first time until two weeks ago."

"Did you just move here?"

"Yeah, but it's not that. It's a Holy Spirit thing. I am called to this place." He laughed a sniggering, adolescent laugh.

This completely unnerved my spiritually evolved self: a hugely overweight stranger with a Beavis and Butt-Head laugh who seemed enamored of the cemetery.

I got a pen out of my purse, to use as a weapon should the need arise.

"Dust to dust!" he enthused. I smiled, rather grimly, and reminded myself to breathe slowly. If you want to feel loving, I coached myself, do something loving. This is basic soul care.

I don't even know what that means — soul. Traditionally it is believed to be the component of ourselves that survives physical death; a reflection of the Holy, made up of light and breath and silence and love, of everything ancient and of babies about to be born. C. S. Lewis said, "You don't have a soul. You *are* a soul. You have a body." If this is right, we have a purpose, which is to shine, like the moon shining in the sky; or to paraphrase the old bumper sticker: Think globally, shine locally.

So I tried, through clenched teeth, to shine.

I offered him gum, the Communion of Dentyne. We chewed gum together and listened to the classical station: instant church. The music was beautiful, now a Bach partita, but I wasn't riveted as before with the Mozart, when I'd felt the thing inside me come to pure attention, a dog being offered bacon. I used to imagine the soul as the gentle intelligent energy at the steering wheel of my body, until I realized that the driver of me was usually late and punitive on the road. Then for a while I saw it as the one-year-old cartoon baby Maggie Simpson, attentive and good, until I shared my insight with Sam, who snapped, "Oh my *God,* Mom. I guess you forgot that she shot Mr. Burns." I love Gerard Manley Hopkins's line about the soul, "the dearest freshness deep down things," and that seems pretty close. But lately I'd been imagining it also as a baby kangaroo, several months old, peering over its mother's pouch with big peepers at the world, as she carried it around, infinitely safe.

Highway 280 became 19th Avenue, the main road to the Golden Gate Bridge, and led past San Francisco State, where in the sixties my dad took us to rallies at which students and professors protested Sam Hay-akawa's tenure, past all the places on 19th where my tennis partners and I used to hang out after long mornings on the public courts. And then, right before 19th swerves sharply to become 13th, or Park Presidio, the driver made a sudden left into Golden Gate Park.

"What are you doing?" I asked.

"I know a shortcut," he said. He turned off the radio, which, since the cemetery, had been my main signal to okayness. Without it, panic flared inside me.

"There is no shortcut — Nineteenth Avenue is the shortest way! What are you doing?" I asked again, really afraid. I could see, in the streetlight from the deserted boulevard, his long, fat fingers gripping the steering wheel: his long, strangly fingers.

He laughed. "Oops," he said, and laughed his Beavis and Butt-Head laugh.

It was like an elevator making an ominous sound. Thick trees overhung the road and blocked out the moon. I had no water with me, and my mouth was dry, my tongue like Velcro. The driver looked at me in the rear-view mirror. I wanted to scream: it was so dark, his hands were so huge, and I was so alone.

"What are you doing?" I asked again.

"Someone told me about a shortcut," he said.

As we drove deeper into the dark, desolate woods, I said sharply, "You must go back to Nineteenth Avenue."

But he kept on driving.

And he stopped talking to me.

"Excuse me," I said. "Excuse me!" I would have called the cops, but I didn't have a cell phone. I thought about borrowing his, as a test: if he lent it to me, it meant I didn't have to call the cops. If he didn't, then I'd leap out of the car. But I just sat tight; so tight; tight as a sphincter.

We had been only ten minutes from the bridge, and now we were in no-man's-land. I'd been in the picnic fields here once the previous summer for a John Kerry fundraiser, but before then I hadn't been to the west side of the park that often in the thirty-plus years since I was a teenager, when my friends and I used to hitchhike to hear the Grateful Dead and Jefferson Airplane. I'd taken Sam to the other side of the park many times when he was young, to the same places my father used to take me — Stow Lake for paddleboat rides, the crocodile pit inside the Academy of Sciences, the Japanese Tea Garden, the de Young Museum, peace marches that ended up in the Haight-

Ashbury — but I hadn't brought Sam to this side of the park, because there wasn't that much going on, even during the day.

The car now passed the deserted picnic grounds, and then the barbecue pits, which made me think of the teenage boy in Marin who years ago killed his parents and burned the bodies in their backyard barbecue pit. But the driver did not stop to burn me up. Instead, he kept driving until we reached the buffalo paddocks. This felt like something of an improvement: I'd loved this place when I was a small child. As a teenager, I used to come here with friends after school to smoke dope. The buffalo were always milling around their meadow, which they shared with red-winged blackbirds and regular old blackbirds and the occasional red-tailed hawk. Things could change on a dime when you were stoned. You might be blissing out on the park's beauty and your deeply developed Native American connection to the Great Spirit, communing with one of the buffalo, feeling that it was talking to you: "Hello, Sister Mammal," it would say. Then all at once you'd be tweaking and think the buffalo were going to come roaring toward you, their mouths open wide, like grizzlies.

The driver pulled over. I thought about

jumping out of the car, but I had no phone, and there was nothing but deserted darkness around, and God only knows what dangers lurked in the shadows.

Plus, my laptop was in the trunk. Also my toiletries and medications. My products.

Without a phone or the courage to leap from the car, I did the only things I could think of: first I got out my car key and clutched it in my right hand, the pen still in my left, and then I prayed, the great Helping Prayer, which goes: "Helphelphelphelp. Helphelphelphelp."

And right then the driver reached for his cell phone and made a call. "I need to talk with my dispatcher," he said. I nearly swooned with relief. Then I heard a busy signal at the other end. If he said hello to the busy signal, I would know to leap out of the car. But he hung up and resumed driving.

"Helphelphelphelp," I prayed again, but instead of feeling Jesus beside me, I could sense only the lunatic employees of the Swing Shift. This is the committee inside me that is sometimes dumb and dangerous with bad judgment, and often obsessed with thoughts of personal greatness or impending doom. Like, for instance, the unbearable truth that all the people you love most will die, maybe in painful circumstances, and soon, probably sometime next week. I hugged my arms to my chest, with the key and the pen tucked inside my armpits, my wet and swampy armpits, my crocodile-pond armpits. The driver veered abruptly to the left, onto the street that takes you out of the park to 41st, still under tall trees but with the streetlights of the avenues just ahead.

"Excuse me!" I said. "Try the dispatcher again."

"I think I know where I am now," he replied.

There were no shops or gas stations, just houses with their lights out. The Swing Shift kept telling me that I could outrun the driver if I leapt out of the car, unless I was too badly injured — but where on earth would I go? I could feel Jesus next to me with his little glow-light, which reminded me of what my pastor Veronica always says: "In life and in death, we are God's — there is nowhere we can be where God isn't with us," which she always says with a perfectly straight face. This helped, for a moment: as Father Tom says, every year you've been in recovery buys you one second of sanity in a crisis. So I was able to calm myself for twenty seconds.

When the bell rang at twenty seconds, though, I became the joey in its mother's pouch, only instead of feeling safety, I felt the mother kangaroo's terror at a nearby threat, a big red-mouthed danger.

Jesus reminded me that he was with me always, here, now.

The Swing Shift noted helpfully that if my leg was crushed while I leapt from the car, I would get to take serious narcotics.

But then, out of nowhere, I felt my furious girl inside me. I'd known her for only three weeks, since a day in church when, during silent prayers, an apparition surprised me. Two feet away stood a teenage girl, trying to claw and scratch my face, held back by an adult woman I didn't recognize. I drew away, because I could honestly feel her, this girl I suddenly and absolutely knew was me. Her hair was not mine, it was longer, and only slightly curly, and it kept me from seeing her face, but I knew she was raging at me, and that she was actually there. I can't explain it better than that. (I also feel a real true wife who lives in me, and I experience her coming to me, the same way I experienced Jesus hunkered down in a corner of my houseboat late one night the year before I got sober). I'm not crazy, or at least this is not a symptom of craziness. I know from distortion and illusion; I know sometimes when you're hiking in the fog or at dusk you think you see the most startling thing and your mind makes up stories to explain it. My hiking friend Judy once thought she saw a moose on the road, but it turned out to be a big dog carrying an unimaginably large branch in its mouth, twigs reaching up from both sides. In church, however, I recognized the furious girl instantly, although I had never seen her before. I understood in a blink that she was someone I had ignored or kept hidden all my life. Later that day I figured out that I wouldn't have been a decent writer without her, and ever since I made that connection, I have felt her presence off and on, lingering there in the shadows.

I thought about her now in the car.

And I could see that she was not happy with this situation.

I sat holding the pen in my left hand, the key in my right, as we drove through the dark streets. There were about ten of us passengers by then: me, the furious girl, Jesus there with his nice glow stick, the two petrified kangaroos, and the Swing Shift, all jumbled together, the way entire litters of children used to be allowed to occupy the back, with no seat belts. I still felt terrified, but not alone. Then I felt myself as a high school girl watching the buffalo thirty-five years earlier, convinced in her stoned fear that they might attack and trample her. And I wondered, for another twenty seconds, if my huge driver was actually as benign as those buffalo.

Then I found myself sitting with Jesus and the furious girl, clutching my weapons, but the Swing Shift was gone, and some of me was semi-okay. The driver now picked up his phone again. I held my breath as he explained where we were. I could hear the man on the other end chewing him out, and part of me panicked. Don't be an ass, you'll push him right over the edge, I thought. And part of me felt for him, this huge guy new to the city, new to this job. He listened. He kept saying, "Right. Right."

Then he hung up. "The dispatcher says we're near the Great Highway. We can get to the bridge through the Presidio." Five minutes earlier, the Swing Shift would have shoved me out of the car at the word "Presidio," which is as dark as the grave. But the Swing Shift wasn't on duty anymore, and the Night Shift is so much more stable: they are on duty when the lights on the ward are low, and most of the patients asleep.

"Sounds like a plan."

When we reached the highway, a shard of moon was shining on the ocean waves. "Boy, talk about not getting off on a good foot with the *boss*," he mumbled, and sniggered into his chest, but by then we were driving north again, and I was heading home.

I got us each some more gum, and we talked all the way past the ocean, through the Presidio, across the bridge, and past the hills of Sausalito. I pointed out my church to him, like a kid, when we passed Marin City. You can see it from the highway. My heart was lifted by seeing it, even in the dark. When I get there on Sundays and pass the room where the choir rehearses, I can hear their muffled voices behind the closed door. I love hearing them, no matter how hushed, but every so often, one of them has to leave practice for a moment and opens the door just as I am passing by, and a beam of singing falls directly on me.

The Last Story of Spring

One day last May, I was heading home after dropping my son off at school. Sam had said the most unexpected thing: I'd asked how he'd liked *Macbeth,* which his sophomore English class had just finished. "I didn't love it," he told me. When pressed, he added, "I had no idea it would be *so* tragic." I thought of that as I drove along, about how many friends of mine are face-to-face these days with the truth of this, and how the rest of us are merely feeling deeply in the generic dark, about our teenagers, our bodies, and Bush.

I started making the turn onto my own street, but without exactly meaning to, I swerved back onto the main road. I call this a Holy Spirit snatch, when something inside you clears its throat, tugs on your sleeve, or actually takes the wheel. When I asked Father Tom where we find God in this present darkness, he said that God is in creation, and to get outdoors as much as you can. So a few minutes after I turned away from home, my big dog and I were in the parking lot beneath the foothills of Mount Tam.

Lily bounded ahead on the path. The air smelled grassy and warm and clean, like oats that had just come out of the dryer. There was a mild breeze that did not have an objective, the way the biting winds of winter do. It was breathing the cool air, too, draping you lightly in itself.

A riot of wild flowers lined our way up the narrow path on the hillside. Lily raced around, carrying branches in her mouth, such a danger running past me that I had to keep stepping aside like a matador to avoid being whacked. Most of the wild flowers now were purple and orange, monkey flowers and lupine and of course, poppies, the traffic cones of a foothill meadow.

The mountain iris seem to stick mostly to themselves. They are not as showy as the irises in my garden: they are the color of old-fashioned ladies' face powder, almost lambent. They are so stately compared with all the purple flowers, the scruffy weeds, and the big thrusting, shouting pom-pom girls.

Lily ran off with her sticks, bounded up

the steep hillside, then doubled back to check in with me. She loves me the way I love Jesus, falling into a trance of despair when she can't feel me. My brother says that whenever he stays with her in the car when I go into a store, she stares at the store as if it were on fire, and then at him, desperately, like, "Can you please take me in there?"

Under the canopy of trees on the hillside, light and shade dappled the path, so it looked like a leopard's coat. When Lily and I had walked another fifteen minutes, we left the woods and came out to the sunny flanks of the hills. We were both panting. The difference is that Lily tore off farther up the mountain, whereas I gripped my side and plopped down on the trail. The meadows were crazy jumbles of flowers, giddy experiments of a painter trying ideas out together: How about this with this — isn't it wiggy? The sweep of foliage at the top of the hill, bunchy and fleecy and furry, rolled like a body, with haunches and shoulders, knees and a belly. It kept its shape, but was generous. Resting, I let my vision blur, and practiced looking out of the corners of my eyes. After the 2004 presidential election, Tom told me that according to a friend of his, during times of darkness, you need to develop night vision; if you look straight ahead in the dark, directly at things, you often see only looming shapes, and you're likely to get blindsided. So you need to look at things out of the corners of your eyes — shapes, positions, objects in relief and in relationship to one another. You may still not see perfectly, but it will be enough to see by and in time it will help you know what is true; as Veronica said, Easter means you can put the truth in a grave but you can't keep it there. Out of the corners of your eyes means, in real life, that you listen to your intuition, hunch, faith.

While I was practicing seeing glimmers and suggestions and shapes, I realized Lily was missing. She sometimes runs off through the chaparral and returns when I call, but this time she didn't. At first I wasn't worried. I could see the whole world from where I sat. I had some quiet minutes of calling for her, expecting her to burst out of the brush at any moment. I scanned the trails above and below me, and a fire road down the hill that drops off suddenly, like something Wile E. Coyote might tear off from, pedaling like mad in midair for a few seconds before looking down.

After a while, though, I realized Lily was really gone, and panic set in. What if I had to go home without her, had to get into my car alone in the parking lot, with one last look? What if I had to tell Sam? Then I thought of Lily's lonely death on the mountain. I thought of wolves eating her.

Losing Lily would be the end of the world, in a way you can understand only if you know what a dear, precious being she is, or if you have a dog you adore, or if, like us, you have just barely, within the last few years, survived the loss of another dog.

I started walking about more quickly, calling for her, clapping, but no Lily. Then, way below me, down on the stretch of fire road, I saw a squirrel race toward where the road drops off, skipping like a pebble on water, faster than a speeding bullet. A minute or so later, from out of nowhere, I saw Lily bolt onto the same road, heading for the dropoff: "Good smell! Over there! Oh, my!"

But as I started running down the hill after her and before she hit the dropoff, she veered off to the right and disappeared down the side of the mountain I call the Canyon of Death. I made my boyfriend walk there once with me, and we are still trying to get over it. There is no path through the brush; it is dark and shadowy and steep and leads nowhere, except to where a modern Bluebeard might bury his wives.

I called and called, but I was too far from her. I ran toward the Canyon of Death and thought about all the mountain lions here, and the coyotes. And the rattlesnakes. I prayed as I ran, but Lily was not there when I got to the fire road. So again I clapped, and called, and prayed. Then I remembered teaching Sam that if you get lost, stay put, so I stood still, and ran through every one of my skills, deficiencies, mental problems, and faith, all in the course of five minutes.

But still no Lily. I looked around wildly. All I can say is that I didn't go into the total panic that would have hurt me physically, like rushing down the hillside into the Canyon of Death. God! When did I start worrying about falling down and breaking my hips? I'll tell you — about three days after my skin cleared up, in my late thirties.

I stayed put and called for her. It occurred to me that it was I who was lost, not Lily — I was so lost in the fear of loss, in the knowledge of all the places where the people and animals I love can go, where I can't follow. Like teenage Sam, and now Lily. As is usually the case — which I totally resent — I couldn't fix or save anything. I'm not a tracker. I'm just someone who loves a dog.

194

All I could do was pray to stay calm, and hope that someone useful might appear. An EMT. Or a ranger. Or some scouts.

If I had been where there was an obvious place to begin a search-and-rescue effort, I might have started there, but I wasn't. I could not be in my usual clunky, overly game, charge-ahead body. But because I couldn't bash my way through anything, I looked for spaces — out of the corners of my eyes.

And right where the sky opened, in the space where the fire road dropped off, the last person on earth I was expecting came along. It was Amanda, an old friend I bump into now and then. She had been sad the last few times I'd run into her, as she was going through a divorce after many years of marriage. She was with her golden retriever, Rocket, only five but already seriously arthritic, limping behind her.

Amanda called out ecstatically. This was a "godsend," she said, because she so needed to talk.

I walked toward her with my arms open for a hug, trying to figure out how to get rid of her so I could look for Lily.

Amanda is usually the person to whom you turn when things are hard, but on this day she came with a heavy load of her own troubles. Taking apart a life with someone else is never much fun, especially with a child still at home, even when both parties feel it is the right thing to do. She told me that she was renting a U-Haul that afternoon to take her things out of the house that she'd shared with her husband and where she'd raised her child; she had a week until the realtors started showing the place. Rocket gimped around like Walter Brennan. I couldn't tell her that I didn't have time to listen because Lily was missing. When she finally took a breath, though, I did.

Amanda started clapping, which is how we call Lily. "Come on, Rocket," she exhorted, as if the dog worked K-9 for the FBI, but by now he was lying down, gasping.

"I think I'll run down to the parking lot and check," I said.

"No, no, we're going to help you. Aren't we, Rocket!" It was ridiculous. We walked around the fire trail, clapping, calling, the panic and grief in me rising. My enchanted woods had turned into the dark forests of fairy tales. But looking at Amanda out of the corners of my eyes, I remembered what happens in fairy tales: The helper always appears in a form that doesn't look very helpful, yet that's who's going to get you out of the woods. In fairy tales you have to stay open to the search, and to goodness and generosity. So I tried to be that way, even though I wanted to yank Amanda and Rocket and get them to race around with me. But Rocket was not at all yankable at that point — he looked as if he needed a stretcher. So I was forced to be patient.

We stayed put on the fire road, intermittently clapping and calling for Lily, while Amanda told me more about the U-Haul project. I listened. And that must have been enough for *something* to happen — call it grace or magic or answered prayer or coincidence — but because I was *exactly* where I was, not down in the Canyon of Death or heading to the parking lot, I was there when Lily appeared. All of a sudden, out of the corners of my eyes, I could see her, far away, at the top of a hill, like Rin Tin Tin. I cried out for her and Amanda clapped, and Lily bolted toward us.

She eventually reached us, panting, the inside of her mouth dark with dirt, and after I chastised her and cried a little, and after Rocket leapt to his feet and threw himself at her, the four of us headed down the mountain. We walked toward the parking lot, so happy that we were not walking into the abyss; not today. I harangued a promise from Amanda that she would call our vet, Rob, who practices Eastern and Western medicine and has healed a number of our friends' hopeless cases. My uncle Ben told me when I turned twenty-one that God works in mysterious ways Her tum-tum to perform, and apparently so does Rob. As it turned out, he had a cancellation that very afternoon, and saw Rocket that day for the first of a dozen treatments, after which, as God is my witness, Rocket did not even have a trace of a limp.

Tiny white wild flowers grew in the grass, and clover lined the trail as at a girl's First Communion. We reached an awning of eucalyptus and redwood, where it was much cooler, and stopped to listen to the sounds of the creek: a steady deep burble, like a water engine, running and pouring over the rocks, and the rocks singing.

■ ■ ■ ■

SAMWHEEL

■ ■ ■ ■

A man riding on the meaning of rivers
Sang to me from the cloud of the world:
Are you born? Are you born?
— Muriel Rukeyser
from "Are You Born? — 1"

CHIRREN

By the time my child was born, I had seen two ultrasound images of him. He looked like a very nice person: perfect, helpless, sleeping. I love that in a baby. I thought about him every few minutes during my pregnancy, talked to him, imagined our conversations as he grew, and lived for his arrival.

But during labor, I began to realize how hard it was going to be without a partner or any money or an overabundance of maternal instincts. Also, that I did not like to spend time with children all that much.

By then, of course, it was too late to reconsider why I wanted to have a child. Midway through the birth process, there was no way out — I couldn't say, "Let's just skip it. I have to go home now." This is the reason most first children get born: By the time it's too late to back out, you have already fallen desperately, pathetically in love with them. For too long, I had imagined holding him, smelling him, watching him grow; teaching him and reading to him, and walking and studying and resting and splashing around in the ocean with him, and comparing notes with him on the mean children in the park.

I loved him intimately, sight unseen. Yet when he lay on my chest for the first time, part of me felt as if someone had given me a Martian baby to raise, or a Martian puppy. And I had no owner's manual, no energy, no clue as to what I was supposed to do.

The other part of me felt as though I were holding my own soul.

Now, all these years later, this still pretty much says it.

Why did I, like many other single women, many gay men and women, many older women, and many other not-so-obvious parents, people who used to think they could never have kids, choose to do so?

Let me say that not one part of me thinks you need to have children to be complete, to know parts of yourself that cannot be known any other way. People with children like to think this, although if you are not a parent, they hide it — their belief that having a child legitimizes them somehow, validates their psychic parking tickets. They tell pregnant women and couples and one another that those who have chosen not to breed can never know what real love is, what selflessness really means. They like to say that having a child taught them about authenticity.

This is a total crock. Many of the most shut-down, narcissistic, selfish people on earth have children. Many of the most evolved — the richest in spirit, the most giving — choose not to. The exact same chances for awakening, for personal restoration and connection, exist for breeders and nonbreeders alike.

But some of us unlikely candidates did have children, and this is why I did:

Instinct, and all that. As for so many women, my body said, Do it. My body kept looking at the watch on its wrist and moaning with worry. But parenthood is also a modus vivendi, an arrangement where people finally know or think they know what it's all about: You've had a kid, your destiny has arrived, you're busy with extremely important things, and you're too committed and tired to pursue the petty obsessions you used to have.

I had never had a particularly strong craving to procreate, except for earlier fantasies of wanting to be Marmee in *Little Women,* which, of course, was really a desperate longing to *have* a mother like Marmee, who cuddled endlessly and kept her weight down. Yet I somehow always assumed I would be a mother. I had a couple of abortions in my twenties, not because it would have been inconvenient for me to have a child, but because I was single, habitually broke, nomadic, and a practicing alcoholic. These abortions brought me anguish, but also the profound relief that they were the right and sane courses to take. Even so, I felt more and more of a longing to have a child someday. It was almost a calling, like the inexorable pull toward the life of a priest or a nun or a poet.

When I got pregnant at thirty-four, my assumption that I would be a mother dovetailed with the knowledge that it would be increasingly harder to conceive if too many more years passed. I might not ever get pregnant again. I was still single, habitually broke, nomadic, but by now I was three years sober and finally beginning to grow up. So I went forward with my pregnancy, with fear and anticipation and a shyness, too, in the face of the enormity of becoming a parent.

I had my friends' love, and great relatives

— especially my younger brother, who lived down the street from me — and I knew, trusted, believed, and hoped a lot of things.

My faith told me that my child and I would be covered, that God's love, as expressed in the love of my friends and family, would provide for us one hundred percent of the time. This turned out to be true. God was most show-offy when things did not go according to my plans, which was approximately ninety percent of the time.

A sober friend told me that while fear and confusion often swirl around us, faith is straight ahead: I trusted that even though I didn't know a thing about taking care of infants, toddlers, kids, or teenagers, I would be shown the next right step on a need-to-know basis. I trusted that other parents would help me every step of the way, and that if I did not keep secrets when motherhood was going particularly badly, there would be healing and enough understanding and stamina to get by. And this has proven to be true.

I thought that there would be a little more downtime. That's a good one.

I believed that at some point rather early on, a quiet confidence would inform me, and it did sometimes. But I was stunned by how afraid I felt all the time, too. My friend Ethan says that being a parent means you go through life with the invisible muzzle of a gun held to your head. You may have the greatest joy you ever dreamed of, but you will never again draw an untroubled breath.

I thought a lot of things: There would be some sort of deep communion between me and my child, a fleshy communion of delicious skin on mine, of smells and textures and silences. This bond would be so rich and deep and intuitive that my lifelong quest for a sense of connectedness would at last be over. Much of this was fantasy, the longing of a lonely, scared child. But there was and is the experience of truly twining with another human soul. And there was soft, unarmored baby skin, and that was priceless, and there was also much juiciness in our bond — although I was unprepared for what uncomfortable juice it would be, and how it came with such lumps and grit in it.

I believed that being a parent would be a more glorious circuit than it's turned out to be — that the transmission would be more reliable. Now I think I imagined it would be more like being a *grand*parent. It's been a lot of starts, stops, lurching, and coasting, and then braking, barely in control, gears grinding, and then easing forward.

I knew that children could teach you how to pay attention, but by the same token so can shingles, and I knew that children gave you so many excuses to celebrate, only half of them false. You will have to forgive me for using these terms: Children can connect you to the child inside you, who can still play and be silly and helpless and needy and capable of wonder. This child does not have to be yours, of course. It can be a niece or nephew, or the child of a friend. But living with a child makes the opportunity for this more likely. Having a child, loving a child deeply in a daily way, forces you to connect with your mortality, forces you to dig into places within that you have rarely had to confront before, unless you have taken care of a dying parent or friend. What I found way down deep by caring for my father during his illness and then by having a child is a kind of eternity, a capacity for — and reserves of — love and sacrifice that blew my mind. But I also found the stuff inside me that is pretty miserable. I was brought face-to-face with a fun-house mirror of all the grasping, cowardly, manipulative, greedy parts of me, too.

I remember staring at my son endlessly when he was an infant, stunned by his very existence, wondering where on earth he had come from. Now when I watch him sleep, I know that he somehow came from life, only I cannot put it into words any better than that.

SAMWHEEL

There are only six stories about Sam at seventeen that he'll allow me to tell, and this is my favorite. It's about a fight we had once that left me wondering whether anyone in history had ever been a worse parent or raised such a horrible child. It challenged my belief that there is meaning to life, and that we are children of divine intelligence and design.

Our fight was ostensibly about the car. We have an old beater that I let Sam drive whenever he wants, although because I pay for the insurance I have some leverage. It's a good deal for him. But I had taken away his car privileges earlier in the week because he'd been driving recklessly, hit a curb going twenty, and destroyed the front tire. So he felt mad and victimized to begin with, my big, handsome, brown-eyed son. And actually, so did I. I asked him to wash both cars, as partial payment for the tire I'd had to buy. It was a beautiful sunny day, and he had other plans, which I made him postpone. I went for a walk with the dog, to let him work in peace. When I got back, the cars were still gauzy with dirt.

I pointed this out as nicely as possible.

"I washed them," Sam said defiantly.

"You liar," I said in an affectionate way, because his response was so flagrantly not true that I assumed he was joking.

He produced two filthy washrags. "I'm not a liar," he said. "I just did a lousy job." Turning to walk away, he looked back and gave me a catalytic sneer.

It was as if something had tripped a spring-loaded bar in me. And for the first time in our lives, I slapped him on the face.

He didn't flinch — in fact, he barely seemed to register it. He gave me a flat, lifeless look, and I knew that I was a doomed human being, and that neither of us could ever forgive me.

Then I grounded him for the night.

I felt I had no choice. Slapping him did not neutralize his culpability: it simply augmented mine.

He looked at me with scorn. "I don't care what you do or don't do anymore," he said. "You have no power over me."

This is not strictly true. He has little

money of his own and loves having our old car to tool around in. Also, he realizes that families are not democracies, and he's smart enough to obey most of the time.

We stood in the driveway, looking daggers at each other. The tension was like the air before lightning. The cat ran for her life. The dog wrung her hands.

I felt a wall of tears approaching the shore, and without another thought, I got in my car and left. Nothing makes me angrier, nothing makes me feel more hopeless, than when someone robs me of my reality by trying to gaslight me. Like Charles Boyer with Ingrid Bergman, saying he hadn't seen her purse, when actually he'd hidden it. Or lowering the gas jets and then pretending not to notice the darkness. I started to cry, hard, and not long after, to keen, like an Irishwoman with a son missing at sea.

Recently I have begun to feel that the boy I loved is gone, and in his place is this male person who pushes my buttons with his moodiness, scorn, and flamboyant laziness. People tell me that the boy will return, but some days that is impossible to imagine. And we were doing so well for a while, all those years until his junior year of high school, when the tectonic plates shifted inside him. I've loved him and given him so much more than I've ever given anyone else, and I'll tell you, a fat lot of good it does these days.

I should not have been driving, but since I'd restricted Sam's driving privileges, I couldn't make him leave. So I drove along, a bib of tears and drool forming on my T-shirt. Why was he sabotaging himself like this, giving up his weekend, his freedom, and his car, and for what? Well, this is what teenagers have to do, because otherwise they would never be able to leave home and go off to become their own people. Kids who are very close to their parents often become the worst shits, and they have to make the parents the villains so they can break free without having it hurt too much. Otherwise, the parents would have to throw rocks at them to get them out of the house. It would be like a TV wilderness show where the family has nursed the wounded animal back to health, and tries to release it into the wild, shooing it away: "Go ahead, Betty! You can fly!"

So even though, or because, I understood this, I cried harder as I drove, harder than I have since my father died. God invented cars to help kids separate from their parents. I have never hated my son as much as when I was teaching him to drive. There, I've said it, I hated him. Sue me: it's actually legal, and sometimes he hates me, too. He always drove too fast, cut corners too sharply, whipped around in the '95 Honda like it was a souped-up Mustang convertible. But somehow he tricked the California Department of Motor Vehicles into issuing him a license. I hate the way most young men drive, so cocky, reckless, apparently entitled. I suppose they hate the way I drive, too — slow and careful, all but shaking my puny fist at them as they pass.

I started letting Sam drive himself to and from school, and to and from his appointments, events, practices. I also ordered him to make emergency runs for milk and ice cream sundaes. But recently as he was leaving, I saw him peel around the corner nearest to our home, endangering himself and anyone who might have been on the street. I threatened to take away his driving privileges, and he slowed down. For two days. Then he sped up when he thought I wasn't looking, and lost his rights for a week.

What has happened? Who is this person? He used to be so sane and positive, so proud of himself. He used to call himself "Sam-wheel" when he was five, because while he couldn't pronounce "Samuel," he knew it was a distinguished name. He used to care about everything, but now he seems to care only about his friends, computers, music, and most hideously, his cell phone — the adolescent's pacemaker. He threatens to run away, because he wants his freedom, and the truth is, he is too old to be living with me anymore. He wants to have his own house, and hours, and life. He wants my permission to smoke, so he doesn't have to sneak around. He wants to stay out late, and sleep in, and because I won't let him do any of this on weekdays, he sees me as a prig at best and at worst a coldhearted guard at Guantánamo.

I wept at the wheel on a busy boulevard. At first people were looking over at me as they passed in the next lane. I wiped at my face and snorfled. Then I noticed that people were dropping back. Eventually, there were no cars in my immediate vicinity. I felt like O.J. in his Bronco on that famous ride. I started calling out to God, "Help me! Help me! I'm calling on you! I hate myself, I hate my son!" I wanted to die. What is the point? What if the old bumper sticker is right and the hokey-pokey *is* what it's all about?

But I have to believe that Jesus prefers honesty to anything else. I was saying, "Here's who I am," and that is where most improvement has to begin.

You've got to wonder what Jesus was like at seventeen. They don't even talk about it in the Bible, he was apparently so awful.

Then I said the stupidest thing to God: I said, "I'll do anything you say."

Now this always gets Jesus' attention. I could feel him look over, sideways, and steeple his fingers. And smile, that pleased-with-himself smile. "Good," I heard him say. "Now you're talking. So go home already, and deal with it."

So I drove home, wiping at my eyes, and when I stepped inside, Sam said, his voice dripping with contempt, "What do *you* have to cry about?"

I staggered to my room, like Snagglepuss onstage. I sat on the floor and thought about his question. The answer was, I didn't have a clue. But all the honest parents I know — all three of them — are in similiar straits.

Their kids are mouthy now, and worse: they couldn't care less about school, and some are barely passing. They drive like movie stars from the fifties, like Marlon Brando or Troy Donahue. You can see in their driving that everything in them is raw, too intent, and thoughtless. No wonder teenagers make such good terrorists.

And me? I think it was all over the moment Sam was born. I recognized that the things I hated about my parents — their fixation with our doing homework and getting into a good college; their need to show us off and make us perform socially for their friends — were going to be things Sam hated about me someday. I also knew that I would wreck his life in ways my parents couldn't have even imagined. I knew that God had given me an impossible task, and that I would fail. I knew deep down that life can be a wretched business, and no one, not even Sam, gets out alive.

It turns out that all kids have this one tiny inbred glitch: they have their own sin, their own stains, their own will. Putting aside for a moment the divine truth of their natures, all of them are wrecked, just like the rest of us. That is the fly in the ointment, and this, Sam, is what I had to cry about.

When I finally stopped my sobbing, I called Father Tom, who is one of Sam's dear friends, too. I told him my version. He listened.

"You're right on schedule," he said. "And so is he. And I was worse."

"You swear? Thank you! But it's still hopeless. What should I do?"

"Call the White House and volunteer him

216

for the National Guard."

"Anything else?"

"Let the hard feelings pass. Ask for help. Mary and Joseph had some absolutely awful moments, too. See if you can forgive each other a little, just for today. We can't forgive: that's the work of the Spirit. We're too damaged. But we can be willing. And in the meantime, try not to break his fingers."

I sat on my floor and after a while the dog came over and gave me a treatment. Somewhat revived, I tried to figure out the next right thing. It suddenly came to me.

I went and kicked my son's door in.

"Go clean the cars properly," I said. "Now."

And he did, or rather, he hosed them down. Then he went back inside and slammed the door. I went inside and filled a tub with hot soapy water, and took it to him.

"Go wash them again," I said. "With soap, this time. And then rinse them."

I went inside and did everything I could think of that helps when all is hopeless. I ate some yogurt, drank a glass of cool water, and cleaned out a drawer. Then I took my nice clean car to the market and bought supplies: the new *People,* a loaf of wholewheat sourdough, and a jar of raspberry jam. I lay on the couch, read my magazine, and ate toast. Before I started to doze, I turned on CNN softly and watched until I fell asleep.

I woke up a few times. The first time, I was still sad and angry and ashamed, and I knew in my heart that things weren't going to be consistently good for a long time. I was willing for the Spirit to help me forgive myself, and for Sam and me to forgive each other, but these things take time. God does not have a magic wand. I kept my expectations low, which is one of the secrets of life.

When I woke up a second time, I saw the last thing on earth I expected to see: Sam in the room with me, stretched out on the other couch, eating yogurt and watching CNN.

"Hi," I said, but he didn't reply. His legs hung over the side of the couch.

I dozed off again, and when I woke up, he was asleep, the dog on the floor beside him. He was sweating — he always gets hot when he sleeps. He used to nap on this same couch with his head on my legs and ask me to scratch it, and before that, he would crawl into bed beside me and kick off all the covers, and earlier still, he would sleep on my stomach and chest like a hot water bottle. He and the dog were both snoring. Maybe I had been, too, all of us tangled in one another's dreams.

Everything in the room stirred: dust and light, dander and fluff, the air — my life still in daily circulation with this guy I have been resting with for so many years.

BLINK OF AN EYE

One morning about ten years ago I awoke with a savage headache that rendered me unbalanced and nauseated. My six-year-old son came in to see why I wasn't up getting him ready for school. He took one look at the situation — his mother in bed, sweaty and lifeless as the guy in cartoons with X's where his eyes should be — and took charge. Hiking up his pajama bottoms, Sam said, "You go back to sleep. I can get myself ready."

He brought me a glass of orange juice, petted me, the way young children do, and made sounds of sorrow. I got some aspirin out of the nightstand and went back to sleep. When I woke up again, I heard the TV on in the living room, then kitchen sounds. I called out for a progress report. "Doing great, Mom," he answered confidently. "I made my own breakfast."

When I next awoke, with a half-hour until

we would have to leave for school, I called out for an update. "Everything's going great, Mom."

"Have you gotten dressed, honey?"

"Ayyyy-yup," he replied like some old guy from Maine.

So I went back to sleep with a wistful sense of our being partners in this business. Soon Sam would hardly need me at all. After nearly half an hour more of sleep, I bolted out of bed, my headache gone, pulled on clothes, and raced out to gather him for school.

There he sat, on the couch, a root beer in one hand, the TV remote in the other, wearing only his Power Ranger underpants, beaming proudly.

The seasons revolved like a rusty merry-go-round in a schoolyard; he became a young man. Last Sunday morning when I called out to see if Sam was ready to go do some errands, and he said groggily, "Yeah, in a minute," I knew him well enough to go downstairs and check.

He and three other teenagers were in his room, still sleeping, in what smelled like the cafeteria at an elk preserve. One of the friends smokes cigarettes, although not in my house. Another one got busted at school with alcohol and a knife in his backpack. I

221

have known all three boys since they were in first grade, and I adore them. They are bright, sweet, accomplished, and it is always easy to love and accept them, because they are not mine. They gladly help around the house when I ask them to, as Sam does at their houses, and every time I thank them for helping, they shrug like cowboys and say, "No problem."

These days some of Sam's lifelong buddies are in trouble with drugs and alcohol, and so are their girlfriends. One young woman we know is in an institution for the time being. A very young man we know is in rehab in Montana. A few months ago, Sam and I went to the funeral of a local boy who died of an OxyContin overdose: we stood in the chill of an autumn dusk in the old Jewish cemetery in San Rafael, and listened as the boy's mother shoveled the first scoops of dirt onto his coffin. It was the loudest sound I have ever heard.

Most of us have gotten off relatively easy so far — our kids are impossible only half the time, screwing up, troubling our hearts, making dumb choices, forfeiting fragments of their dreams, but still basically okay.

But God, they can be annoying. "Sam," I told him Sunday morning, "you said you'd do errands with me — they're all for you.

222

And your laundry is overflowing — you swore you'd do it yesterday. That's why I let you blow it off the other day. Plus you've got the garbage and the recycling."

"Okay, okay! God." You'd have thought I'd asked him for a pedicure.

John, the young man who got busted at school, opened his eyes and said sleepily, "Hi, Annie." He is often at our house, part of the smelly Jurassic herd who hang out in Sam's room. He's a good person — observant, dignified, funny, and tenderhearted, just like Sam at other people's houses. John has always done wonderfully in school, without much prodding, and it was his and his parents' dream that he would go to a top liberal arts college and pursue a career in journalism; at least, until this semester, when he tanked. Now they hope he can just get in anywhere decent.

I called his father one day in tears, because Sam was in danger of failing a class. John's father and I are allies: he listened, with the tough gentleness only the parent of another great kid in trouble can muster. He expressed love and respect for Sam. Then he said that John had just flunked advanced algebra, and so could not get into any of the UC campuses.

"He's been working for so long to get into

a really good school," said his dad. "And then? It's gone, in the blink of an eye."

Neither of us spoke for a moment. This is obscene, that higher education is so desperately cutthroat that a single adolescent slip can make such a difference in the quality of the rest of a young person's life. He continued haltingly: "It's just the way it is. We talked about it last week when his report card arrived — that what we had all hoped for was probably not going to happen now. It was a sad conversation for both of us. And later that night, when I was in bed, he came into my room and told me, quietly, in the dark, 'Don't give up on me, Dad.'"

His voice cracked. When we hung up some time later, we were both better.

I know what it is like to be scared to death that your child seems out of control, and what it is like when you cannot locate him late at night; I have gotten the two a.m. call from the sheriff's deputy. But I don't know what it feels like to have academic dreams shattered, because our dream has been modest. Sam's always been a good artist, an inventor, an animator, an *imaginator,* but a reluctant student, except for the social life, and art. He had an obvious way with his hands in kindergarten, which is when our troubles began.

His teacher called me one day to schedule a conference, to discuss his problems as a slow paper-cutter. I am not making this up. He was the slowest paper-cutter in the class. The teacher seemed genuinely worried. I pointed out that he was meticulous in his approach to art and numbers, but she wouldn't let go of it. I almost lost my temper. "Why don't you just go ahead and *say* it?" I wanted to shout. "The kid's a loser!"

Yet he and his friends are anything but losers. They are teenagers, wild horses corralled in their parents' homes, who want to carve out their independence; they want to drink, smoke dope, borrow the car.

"Get up, Sam," I told him later Sunday morning. "You've got chores to do — you've already spent your allowance, and you owe me some time. And you promised to go with me to the convalescent home this afternoon."

It was almost noon. I'd decided to skip church, because I'd be performing a service that afternoon at the home, which my church sponsors. "We're not going to have time to do your errands today. I'm going to take Lily for a hike," I said. I wanted to chill out for a while. I told him what I wanted done by the time I got home. We would be leaving at two.

He sat up in bed and rubbed his face. "Okay," he said. "Have a good walk. Bye-bye, Lily."

"Thanks, darling," I said, because his voice was so sweet.

"No problem."

One of the four things I know for sure about raising kids is to savor whatever works. I smiled as his friends woke and surveyed the mess in his room; then I left.

Lily and I set out for our favorite hike on Mount Tamalpais. The contrast was a lovely shock: the mountain and foothills are their own fresh, spacious sacrament for me, especially when the lower hills have begun to turn green. All summer and fall the slopes are golden-brown, and then new green grass appears. It pushes the old grass up and away, until it lies like small hay drifts, gathered neatly before the hay balers arrive. Lily ran ahead, off leash, which is not, strictly speaking — or actually, in any way — legal. But most dogs up here run free. She scampered up the wet grassy hillside. After the rains, the old grass is silvery gray, like a Weimaraner.

I walked along lost in observation of the winter wild flowers beside the path, the lacy moss on tree trunks, the coyote bush on the hillside flocked with white fluff, and was startled by the abrupt appearance of two men. They wore green uniforms, and I knew in a jackhammering heartbeat that they were deputies from the sheriff's department. Just like that, at the point on the path where Mount Tam comes into view, fills the sky and lowlands with green fleecy trees, they stood twenty feet in front of me. I gasped.

"Oh, no," I said, as Lily bounded up to them with a stick in her mouth. They were both in their late thirties or early forties, one nice-looking with a mustache, the other looking a lot like Barney Fife. None of us said anything for a minute. This couldn't be! I'd been on these hillsides many times a week for years now, and I'd never even seen a deputy. And Lily was such a good dog. And I was such a good person, about to head to a convalescent home. God!

The handsome man said, "Looks like you know what we're up to."

I nodded. You hear stories of how they issue $200 fines for not having your dog on a leash. I felt like the teenager in trouble, the deputies my meddling parents. So I instinctively did what I have always done when I've run the tail end of a yellow light, ever since I got my license at sixteen: I worked on a good lie. Then I tried to jolly them out of giving me a ticket — "Could this be like a fix-it ticket, where I show up at your department tomorrow with my dog on a leash? Heeling?"

The first one looked at me sympathetically. The other one stared at me, accusing, hurt.

I hung my head and started to cry. Tears pooled in my eyes — tears of pure adolescent misery and frustration, that years of letting Lily run free were at an end; tears of shame and of simply wanting to be left alone to pursue my life without being hassled to death in one of my favorite places on earth.

Barney got his ticket book out, and then — his mouth drawn as if he were a fierce boy armed with a slingshot — his police radio. I wanted to scream at them: Don't you guys have *anything* better to do? Like arresting the guys in the park who sell drugs to kids? Like busting the old farts outside the movie theater who pick up teenage girls? You're here to hassle and fine a *Greenpeace* supporter?

And it went from bad to worse: "May I see your driver's license, ma'am?" Barney asked. I was lost, furious . . . and olllld.

They did a check for prior convictions and unpaid parking tickets, and I was clean. Barney filled out my ticket and handed it to me. And somehow, I gave up the fight. I sighed deeply, loudly, and shrugged. Then I put on a crafty expression.

"What if I were to tell you that she's not actually my dog?" I asked. The men smiled. I looked at Lily. "I've never seen that dog in my life."

Lily bounded over to me with her branch and flung herself against my leg, staring up at me, a furry, panting Saint John the Divine.

On the lower part of the path home, new grass wasn't growing yet. The short golden grass lay flattened by weather, in swirls of hat hair.

It was after one when I got home. There was progress: Sam was now asleep on the upstairs couch.

I roused him. "We have to leave in an hour," I said. "And I told you to get your chores done before we go."

"Give me ten more minutes!" he cried. And remembering how the cops had made me feel, I let him sleep.

My friend Neshama arrived. She was going with us. I pantomimed choking my sleeping child. Then I made sandwiches for all of us. She and I ate.

At ten of two, I shook Sam again. "Get up

now," I said. I was about to shout at him. But he looked like a skinny marine mammal, washed ashore.

Another of the four things I know for sure about raising kids is that most times when you overlook bad behavior, or let them blow you off when something is important to you, you injure them. You hobble their character.

The third of the four things I know is that if you can shine a small beam of truth on a beloved when you are angry, it is more beneficial than hitting that beloved with a klieg light of feelings and pinning the person to the wall. I can't remember the fourth, but I put numbers 2 and 3 into practice.

I closed my eyes, gathered myself, bent down and spoke to my son calmly.

"Sam? You've said several times you would come with me today. I want you to, but I don't want to make myself crazy trying to get you to live up to your promises. If it doesn't happen, I'm going to be sad and angry, but I am not going to lose myself in your bullshit."

He got up and went downstairs to his room, grumpily. Neshama looked at me.

"You did great," she said. I closed my eyes and let my head drop to my chest. We heard Sam's footsteps on the stairs coming toward us.

The three of us went outside and got in the car, Sam in the backseat, where he ate his sandwich in sleepy silence.

There were only six residents waiting in the recreation room for us to begin the service, five women and one man, fragile as onion skin. There were five of us from church, plus Neshama, so I assigned everyone a resident to shepherd through the short service. We always sing a few songs, say a few prayers, take the residents' hands and look in their eyes and say, "The peace of God be with you." Sam accompanied a pretty Asian woman, who talked to him as if he might be one of her relatives. He introduced himself to her shyly. "Yes," she said happily. "Sam." He took his place at her side. For the next half-hour, he turned the pages of the worship book for her and ran his fingers along the words of each hymn so she could follow. He's been coming here with me off and on his whole life, because I so believe in this ministry and want him to share it with me: the people here are shipwrecks, and sometimes there is not much left, but there is a thread in them that can be pulled and that still vibrates. It's like being with nuns who have taken vows of silence and mutter. So we show up, talk, and sing. It seems to fill the residents, breathe more life into them. Sam's companion beamed and concentrated on doing her part correctly, as if to please him. When we sang "Jesus Loves Me," a song she and the others may have learned as children, some sang along, muttering and murmuring like brooks: there's such pleasure in knowing the words to a song.

I've seen them come back to life during this service, even when they cannot sing. I've seen these moments bring them joy and comfort. We don't lay a heavy Jesus trip on anyone: it's more that he is a medium for our showing up and caring.

My person was sound asleep. I was beginning to think it was the effect I have on people. She was wearing a bright red sweatsuit and could not have weighed more than eighty pounds. When she finally woke up, I greeted her.

"I want to go back to sleep," she cried out, and I assured her that that was okay. I took her hands and she babbled for a minute. "I like that house," she said, and I held on to her hands. Sam came over. "She wants to sleep," he whispered, "because she liked the house in her dreams."

"That's exactly right," I said. He went back to the Asian woman. My woman in red fell asleep again. I continued with a prayer.

Some of the residents seemed to be out of it, drooling, dazed. Then you would hear them saying the Lord's Prayer. *"Amen,"* we say loudly; then we go around one last time, touch each person, and tell them how glad we are that they are there. I realize again and again that this is really all you have to offer people most days, a touch, a moment's gladness. It has to do, and it often does.

"Hey, thanks," I told Sam as we headed outside with Neshama.

"No problem," he said. We walked to my car. "I liked my person," he added. His hair was matted down in bedhead tufts, like the hills.

■ ■ ■ ■

EARTH SCHOOL

■ ■ ■ ■

Perhaps everything terrible is, in its deepest being,
something that needs our love.
— Rainer Maria Rilke

BASTILLE DAY

I'll read anything with the words "divine love" and "impeachment" in the first sentence, so I included them in the first line of my call for a revolution in the spring. I know the word "divine" makes many progressive people run screaming for their lives, and one hesitates to use it. And we all know it's unlikely that there is going to be an impeachment anytime soon. So I hastened to add that this would be a revolution about decency — as in, "Have you no decency?" It would be calm, polite, and inclusive. Perhaps in lieu of "divine love" we could use the idea of "kindness," and we would be guided by the way Gandhi and Dr. King behaved toward the armed white men who fought them when they changed the world.

In the spring of 2006, I believed that good people who had watched their country's leaders skid so far to the triumphal right would want to do something. I mean, wouldn't they? Otherwise, those people's children would ask them someday, when we would all be living in caves, "What did you do to try to save us?" And the children would be angry, and they are so awful and unpleasant when they are mad, even in the dark.

I, for one, did not want to answer that I'd done nothing, or that I'd ranted and flailed, showing up only to support my own causes and candidates. In the face of hate and madness, you can't just turn your face to the wall and give up. I wanted to figure out how to say, "Enough" — and be part of a revolution that would save the world. Or at least help people keep the faith.

I hoped that July 14 worked for everyone.

In 1967, my father published a great novel about an antiwar march, called *The Bastille Day Parade,* in which protesters carry signs that read "Turn Off the Lie Machine." In choosing July 14, I would like to pay tribute to him and to the people of his generation, who are surely turning in their graves with horror about contemporary life in their beloved America. They were passionate in their fight against fascism, Joseph McCarthy, and litterbugs. They were committed to civil rights, to libraries, and to good manners. They raised their children to be polite,

238

as honest as we could manage, and to live as if the word *fair* meant something, which all sounds a little Amish now. A renewal of these values would be the major plank of this revolution.

In this revolution, there would be no positions except greenness, kindness, and libraries. We would not even have a battle cry, as that can lead to chanting and haranguing. We would simply look one another in the eyes, shake our heads, and say, "This can't be right." We would not try to figure out what it all means: Iraq, Guantánamo, Abu Ghraib, Terri Schiavo, abortion rights, the Downing Street memo, domestic spying, immigration, the Kyoto Protocol, the Geneva Conventions, Tom DeLay — none of it.

Mostly we would show up and say things like, "Giving India massive nuclear assistance? I don't know — that just can't be right." Or, "John Bolton at the UN? Jeez, Louise." Also, everyone would commit to taking a few naysayers to Al Gore's movie as the most effective possible consciousness-raising about the ecological tragedy of global warming. We would not suggest through words or body language that George W. Bush's approach to the environment had helped destroy the planet. We would be starting over. We would pass the popcorn.

After an initial call I made in a column for Salon, I was hoping for a large turnout, even though so few people showed up to mark the third anniversary of the invasion of Iraq. This was dispiriting, but let's not dwell on it. More than 59 million people voted for John Kerry, and I was hoping for a turnout somewhere in the neighborhood of 20 million. We would need precinct leaders to get the word out, although not the kind who go door-to-door while people are eating, then threaten sweetly to come back later. Bitter neighbors were the very last thing this revolution sought.

We would all show up on Bastille Day on the biggest street in our town, or in front of city hall, or wherever we felt like gathering, with friends, or alone. We'd be propelled by the ferocious belief we've carried since childhood, that the United States is supposed to be a *republic,* of fifty states, united and humane, and that we'd fight tooth and nail — nicely — for that to be true again.

I thought it would be cool if people turned off their cells phone that day.

I chose a color for the revolution, green, because we've lost our connection with the natural world, and this would be a step toward reclaiming it; also because trees, grass, and the rest of the natural world are incredibly beautiful and precious. Nature is the truth. Some might suspect that this was inching dangerously close to a "position," what with everyone in green, hundreds of shades of green. And if I'm being honest, it's true that the *tiniest* point might be made that a black-and-white worldview, a Manichaean good-versus-evil color scheme, was wearing out its welcome.

We could bring bulbs that we would plant in November, no matter how things shake down. Bulbs are about new life after darkness and storms. It was important that we constantly replant, in case the Bush administration insisted that all daffodils be killed off, under the rubric of the Clean Ground Initiative.

One last thing: It would be great if people brought a bit of fruit to share, and maybe a few dollars, in case anybody ran into someone desperately poor. Bananas are great, as they are the only known cure for existential dread. Also, I've heard that in India, even people dying in the street will share their bananas with anyone who needs them; we might start this tradition of sharing here, too. I once saw a note on someone's computer that said: "The Law of the American

Jungle: Remain calm, and share your bananas." So the more I think about it, the more convinced I am about the bananas.

Jesus would take care of anyone who was hungry, maybe by making soup, and then sitting down to eat with everyone. Then, when people had eaten, he would encourage them to get moving again, and help him pick litter up off the street. But soup is not practical to serve on the day of the revolution. Trust me, fruit is a nice touch. Apples, oranges, it doesn't matter, and it would not be mandatory that you bring fruit at all.

I was asking only that people show up and help foment a revolution based on kindness. Maybe we'd sing "My Country, 'Tis of Thee." No offense in that, is there, if you forget the way the song has been used as a weapon against the people of America, and think instead about the words? "From every mountainside, let freedom ring." Nothing too objectionable, really.

But we wouldn't sing it if doing so would stir up a lot of debate and distraction. I was thinking that both of my parents died here, in this land they loved. They were both born abroad. A lot of our parents have died, people who made sure their children read John Steinbeck, Rachel Carson, and Langston Hughes. I would show up for my parents, by proxy.

Seriously; we wouldn't have to sing that song if it's going to freak people out. Still, I cry when I hear it.

We would come together, on Bastille Day, and ixnay on the cell phones and speeches. As Woody Allen once said before I turned on him, eighty percent of life is simply showing up. We will show up and foment a loving revolution, wearing green: I just looked up *foment,* to make sure that this is what I meant. It comes from the Latin *fomentum,* which means a warm poultice. You apply a cloth, dipped in warm water or medication, to a body that needs healing, and that is exactly what we need to do.

I was thinking noon-ish.

Unfortunately, my plans for the revolution stalled during a book tour in April, although a number of Salon readers around the country shared with me in person that they and their friends were organizing groups of people to show up with them locally on July 14. Then, in late May, when my commitment and strength returned, the weather had turned August-hot. I am not blaming this on the escalation of the earth's destruction during the Bush years. I'm just saying: way too hot for May. And maybe the idea was ridiculous. So I held off on drumming up local support.

On Bastille Day, my feet hurt, and I wondered whether anyone would notice if I sort of skipped the revolution. Also, it was my boyfriend's birthday, and I needed to get to Macy's. I hadn't updated my plans in Salon, because the revolution piece had generated dozens of letters, half of which said it was stupid to stand on the street with a few other aging bleeding-heart-liberal tree-hugging types — like it was a bad thing. Who would be the wiser if I didn't show up, since I hadn't told any of my friends to meet me? But around three I turned on CNN and discovered that the new Israel–Hezbollah conflict was not going as well as one had hoped.

I grew extremely agitated. Years ago I had a button that said: "I'm not worried — I'm just very alert." I sat watching the news in what my grandmother would have called "a state." And then I did the single most important thing one can do to save the world: I got up off my butt.

Even though I had told everyone in my original manifesto that there would be no placards, I felt a nudge in my heart. I got out some poster board and a thick marker, and began drafting. First I wanted to pay tribute to my father by writing, "Turn off the lie machine." Then I thought about plugging *An Inconvenient Truth* because Gore's movie gave me the first hope I'd felt in a decade that this planet could be saved for our children, nieces, nephews. I considered "Pro-Soldier/Pro-Peace," but finally settled on "One People. One Planet. One Future."

I wondered whether those mean readers had been right. Was it stupid?

Then I thought, But everything else is *totally* stupid, on a big scale. The men in power have so screwed things up, hugely. I would be the hermit crab rising up to shake a brave claw.

We need the rising up.

Nothing else can save us.

I kept thinking about the younger people who meet on our main street many nights with signs announcing the latest body counts in Iraq, of both Iraqis and Americans. So I put on a green T-shirt, made my sign, and went to stand under the shade trees downtown.

It was slow at first. I held my sign and smiled, but did not wave the way you do when you have a candidate or a cause to push. When my spirits flagged, I thought about how cheered *I* feel whenever I drive by someone standing up for peace or the environment. This is a plenty good reason to do things.

Still, I felt like a fool — mute, ridiculous, and happy, like Forrest Gump, holding my shitty sign as the world passed by. But you can't go limp in the face of this world's horror and barbarity. Limp is what they want, in the paranoid sense of the word "they."

Finally business picked up. People stared as they drove past, gave me a thumbs-up, a smile, a look of confusion, or a peace sign. Easily half of them were on the phone.

I tried to look at each person kindly, because I believe that we are family. I don't always feel it, but I know it. My pastor Veronica often quotes whoever said that it's not what we're looking at, but what we're looking with, so each crooked smile could be like a minimal dose that, however small, helps the healing. Just as a doctor can help you relax for a moment during a spasm, and you remember you're going to be okay at some point.

I kept telling myself bravely that a small act of peace can cause a quantum shift. Then, after I had been there twenty minutes, I heard a motorized vehicle approach on the sidewalk. I looked over. An old, thin man in an electric wheelchair had paused about ten feet away. I smiled. He wasn't having any of it. He sat there for some time. Then he revved up the motor and scooted to where I stood.

"What are *you* screaming about?" he asked angrily. I stayed neutral, so neutral. I was Sweden, Switzerland. Except for the part of me that thought about pushing him over in his contraption.

"I haven't said a word in over an hour," I replied meekly.

"You should join the Marine Corps," he said with enormous contempt. I looked back at him blankly. I was about to enthuse, "Now *that's* an intriguing idea," when he motored away.

I shook my head and imagined him hiding in the bushes nearby for days, awaiting someone to confront. I couldn't wait to tell my boyfriend.

I stood there until my feet started to hurt. All good revolutionaries ought to invest in a good camp stool. I hated to leave. The tree that shaded me was a sycamore, tall, with an umbrella of manly branches and lush, mapley leaves. The dark bark was peeling, light green emerging underneath.

It was nearly dinnertime when I finally went home, and I was not going to make it to Macy's. I called my boyfriend and told him about my afternoon.

"I'm really sorry," I said.

"The revolution must come first," he said. I poured myself a glass of ice water and turned on the TV. The big new war in the Middle East was more awful by the hour. Some of the pundits were saying it was World War III. What are you supposed to do in the face of this? I pulled out my tree book. The photograph of the sycamore in it looked like the tree that had shaded me. The new bark I'd noticed today, revealed as the old bark fell off, was my favorite color: sea-foam green, the same color as the young harmless snakes around here after they've shed their first skins. I looked up for a moment, and an idea came to me. We had to have another revolution soon. I wondered how mid-October might work for everyone, in the weeks before the midterm elections, when the leaves begin to turn.

Mom, Interrupted

Yesterday, I called my Internet provider with a billing question and got a vivacious female robot who told me how glad she was to help me. Could we begin with my touch-toning my phone number? I hit O for an operator, but this time the robot paused for a second and said calmly, like Nurse Ratched, "Okay — but you'll just have to answer these same questions with someone else. So would you like to begin again, by touch-toning your phone number?"

I could hardly breathe. After a moment, I said, slowly, "Mom?"

My mother has been dead for several years. But old mothers never die, and they never fade away. They are too complicated for either.

For a long time after her death, I didn't feel much of anything — except relief — because I'm a complicated mother, too, and I have my hands full as it is. I felt much more spaciousness in my life after my mother died, partly because my phone did not ring every several seconds, and partly because I didn't have to be both a complicated mother and a complicated daughter at the same time.

My mother was a handful. You can ask her best friends and her sibling: she was imperious, with no self-esteem, which is a terrible combination. She was controlling, judgmental, withholding, needy, and desperate to be loved.

Everyone always said how proud she was of me. But she mostly forgot to mention this to me, and instead held other people's kids up as true successes: people with college degrees, spouses, stylish clothes.

When my mother was alive, I felt like strangling her about half the time. The rest of the time, though, I was tender and dutiful toward her, on every level of her existence, there at her side like an aggrieved bellhop throughout our forty-eight years together. Fortunately, I was still drinking much of that time. Then, after I quit and started to get my life together, she would announce to everyone who would listen that I hadn't been a "real" alcoholic, and that this little phase would pass. For my mother, who had a tiny issue with denial, a real alcoholic meant that you drank like the red-haired lady who lived around the corner from us when I was young, and passed out in the street with some regularity. People in your family were not real alcoholics. They were bons vivants.

I really loved my mother, in a lot of ways. I used to visit her in Hawaii, where she had moved when I was eighteen. I'd agree to visit only if she'd buy marijuana for me from her younger friends. Then, after having several festive blender drinks with her on the lanai, I'd smoke too much dope and become paralyzed while trying to make it to my bedroom — huddling in the hallway and gaping with horror at the two-inch geckos on the wall. Later she would bring me pineapple juice and tuck me in. She was a black-belt co-dependent.

I brought her back from Hawaii when her finances and health began to run out. I took her everywhere, included her every chance I could, and tended to her daily when she got sick with Alzheimer's. She floated away on the riptide of dementia, ultimately a speck on the horizon, waving for as long as she could to her deeply confused children on-shore.

When I think of her, I miss how great it felt to make her laugh — no one could make her laugh harder than I — and last week I had a little episode at the San Francisco airport security line that I long to tell her about. It was such a perfect Nikki story.

I didn't feel like taking off my shoes that day. I had been told by various screeners that taking off your shoes was optional, and on this particular day I chose to exercise my option, since I was wearing flats.

But it turns out to be optional only in the loosest sense of the word. I was verbally nabbed by the screener on the other side of the gate. I was fuming by then, muttering to myself about how they ought to be out there securing our ports, and how if they did that I'd be glad to take off my shoes for them. I was pulled out of the line.

"Look," I said calmly, "I want to know what kind of shoes you don't have to take off." And I swear to God, the screener smirked.

"Try flip-flops," she said, then beamed at the other screeners.

I stood there, all but pawing at the ground like a bull. People in line did not want to make eye contact; I might be a Dr. Scholl's gel bomber. Later, I realized this was a story my mother would have loved. She'd get it: she loved that I was rebellious. (Although she also wished I was married, and rich.)

The "Jesus thing," as she referred to it, just drove her crazy. After I converted, she must have asked herself many times where she'd gone wrong, as she did when I dropped out of college. But one of the innumerable things the Jesus thing gave me was an understanding of how hard it is for all mothers when the time comes for their children to leave.

When Jesus is about twelve, talking to some folks in a temple, a man comes in to tell him that his mother and father are waiting outside for him, and he blows them off.

The man says, "Your mother and father are outside and want to see you." And Jesus says, "Who is my mother? And who is my father?"

But he's trying to say what my son said to me at twelve, and what I said to my mother forty years ago: "Don't you know I'm *twelve* now?" It's wrenching for the mothers, and the drug they use is worry. And their worry is exhausting for kids. It's hard for everyone.

It wasn't until her death that my mother stopped exhausting me. Then I didn't forgive her for a while. All her friends and a few relatives hassled me to let it go, to forgive. But I did it my way, slowly, badly, authentically, eventually scattering her ashes, with deep grief, a year and a half after she died.

Now here it is, three years later, and I am beginning to miss her. Before now, I missed having had a healthier, more elegant mother. But now I miss *her,* Nikki Lamott. I think of her often, and sometimes feel her nearby, the way I feel my father. I think of stories she'd love. I think of how much she must love watching her grandson Sam grow up into a mostly lovely young man, magical and complicated. I think about her being intimately loved by God now, somewhere.

At times I think of her with enormous warmth. The other day, when I walked up the stairs to the house, Sam came out to greet me. He was on the phone and I heard him say, "My mom's home. I gotta go bond." That's how I feel more and more about my mother: that she's home, finally, and I gotta go bond.

JUNCTIONS

I woke up in a bleak place on Sunday. It was not the place of ashes, like the morning after the 2004 presidential election, but there was no comfort anywhere. It was miserably hot, and the news couldn't be worse — a new crop of mutilations in Iraq, with 2,500 U.S soldiers now dead, and a North Korean ICBM apparently pointed at the West Coast. Two of my dearest friends had terrible diseases. There was a nasty separation going on in our family, and a small distraught child. Also, my son had not obeyed his curfew and we had had words at two a.m.

Seventeen can be tough: my friend Meredith said to approach my relationship with Sam like a frozen gym membership, where I am taking a break. So far, I have not pushed him down the stairs, which during rough patches passes for grace around here. This falls short of the heavenly banquet, but some days will have to do.

In the face of all this, I did the most astonishing thing a person can do: I got out of bed. At least I could still walk. A better person would think, Thank you, Jesus. But I thought, *God,* do my feet hurt. God, am I getting old. Then I had some coffee, to level the playing field of me and my mind, as it had had several cups while I slept, and now it felt like talking.

Then I headed to church.

And it was not good.

The service was way long, and boring, and only three people had shown up for the choir, and the song they sang sucked. There was a disruptive baby who had about three hours of neck control but was already spoiling everything for the rest of us. I sat with a look of grim munificence, like so many of your better Christians, exuding mental toxins into the atmosphere. I decided that this church was deteriorating. I had come for a spiritual booster shot and instead got aggravation. I was going to leave, and never come back.

Then something amazing happened. I would call it grace, but then, I'm easy. It was that deeper breath, or pause, or briefly cleaner glasses, that gives us a bit of freedom and relief. I remembered my secular father's only strong spiritual directive: Don't be an asshole, and make sure everybody eats. Veronica quoted a fellow pastor recently: "I'm only a beggar, showing the other beggars where the bread is." There are many kinds of bread: kindness, companionship, besides the flour-and-yeast kind. I remembered Sam at this church in his first months, making loud farting noises with his mouth, or sobbing uncontrollably about the state of things, and no one seemed to care or notice. This memory evoked patience in my anxious, complaining heart. The squalling baby and I tired ourselves out at about the same time. He fell asleep; I pinched the skin of my wrist, to bring myself back to my body. I realized I was going to get through this disappointing service, and anyway, you have to be *somewhere:* better here, where I have heard truth spoken so often, than, say, at the DMV, or home alone, orbiting my own mind. And it's good to be out where others can see you, so you can't be your ghastly, spoiled self. It forces you to act slightly more elegantly, and this improves your thoughts, and thereby the world.

I gave up enough so that my muscles let down, and spent the last hour of the service feeling becalmed in a boat, no paddle, no wind springing up, slightly frustrated. But I knew that there would eventually be movement on the water again, and the wind did pick up toward the end of the service, two hours after it began. Driving home, I no longer felt that I must quit this church as soon as possible, any more than I would quit my family after a disastrous holiday meal.

I went home and read *The New York Times*, usually one of my favorite things, but today it made me crazy. Where will the madness end? The great Andean glaciers are now melting! George Bush's decisions and movements will take a thousand years to recover from, because his people have done such major damage everywhere. We have become a country that you wouldn't want to leave your children alone with.

If all this is happening for a reason, it sure explains a lot of things. In these terrible years since Bush's response to 9/11, I've wondered whether our world is in the throes of labor, the struggle toward the end where all is struggle, contraction, and stuckness, after you remember that you dislike children, but before the doctor lets you start pushing. Maybe a new ice age would be *just* the ticket; and in the meantime, maybe a small volcano blowing up right under Halliburton would be enough to make the company lose stride.

I felt alone and panicky. Sam was still asleep, at two in the afternoon, which is not uncommon for seventeen-year-olds, yet I watched him with tremendous anxiety. I found his drool disturbing. My boyfriend had the flu and was out of commission. My friends were on vacation, except for the one who was doing chemo. It was too hot to sleep, and my only hope was to plug into something bigger than my pulsing mind, to flail around outside rather than within me. God can't clean the house of you when you're still in it. So I went for a walk in the hills with my dog, Lily.

There are always lots of people on the trail I chose that day, because it is legal for dogs to run off leash there, but today there was not a soul on the old fire road. It was too hot. And everything was brown: the hillsides, the grasses, the dirt road. You'd have to be on acid to think it was beautiful up here now. The dusty trails were scrabbly and rocky; I was in constant danger of twisting my ankles. My younger brother saw a long, fat rattlesnake on a trail in these parts the other day. The dry, dusty air smells like chemicals, like pollution, and snakes. It is nature's way of saying, "Go rest in the shade somewhere." I walked along slowly, heavily, while my dog leapt about as if we were in kilts, on the green hillsides of Scotland.

There are purple and lavender wild flowers up here, bleeding hearts and thistles; also buttercups, weedy goldfields, sticky monkey flowers, few and far between. I noticed that people had not been cleaning up after their dogs; there was a lot of product in the road. There are two essential rules up here: No smoking, and Clean up after your dog. What are we coming to? Look at this place, I thought; it's a dump.

I cleaned my glasses on my T-shirt, and considered the situation. There was dust on everything. You'd have needed a home-plate umpire's brush up here to really see things. There was no rain to wash away all the scat. I know this sounds crazy, but it became part of the dust, which then smudged your glasses with atomized snake and finely powdered dog doo. What I counted on daily for pastoral beauty became forsaken and deserted, as it did every summer. There were hair plugs of grass in the dirt. Witchy branches that might reach out and grab your wrist. Abandoned chifforobes would not have looked out of place, tossed from wagon trains by the banded-Calistoga settlers.

I gathered some of the poop with the

plastic bags I had brought to clean up after Lily, and left them by the road for the return trip. When my priest friend Tom is at his most despondent over Bush and global warming, he goes around his neighborhood picking up trash and dog shit. It definitely helps on days when you can't see much hope for this sweet old planet. In the long haul, grace will win out over everything, over the misery, the stupidity, the dishonesty, but it would be so great, so *yoked,* as Sam would say, if our species were around to witness that. Barring revolution, things are going to be very bad for Sam and his children.

An endless wall of live oak cut through the hills like the great wall of China, only you could walk through it like a ghost.

Two people came into view, a handsome young father of maybe forty, with a beautiful and very young Chinese girl in the throes of a tantrum.

She was lying on the trail, wailing, the brat personified. He was attempting to discuss the situation with her. This is always a parent's first line of attack in Marin. I sighed in sympathy. We have all taken turns having the awful, hateful child on display. I felt a moment's relief that it was not my turn. I also thought of all those shins I have wanted to kick all my life, all those parts of me I wish weren't there, all the immature, spoiled parts, shedding brat-cells like skin flakes. The man looked at me and shook his head as his surely beloved child flopped about in the dirt like a fish in the sand. Not so long ago, I had been the girl with pebbles embedded in her back, and my parent hating it so much. I offered the father my bottle of water, which I hadn't opened yet, but he shook his head, so I gave him the only thing I could, a smile: I see you and you see me, and we're both tired, and children can be awful, but did you see the coastal larkspur back there?

After a while, I turned to see how the man and the girl were doing, but they were gone. The hills were silent again except for one birdsong, and it cheered me slightly. See? If there were no other proof of the existence of a bigger reality than birds, they would do it for me.

I started up again, and this time when another person came into sight, my heart quaked. It was a youngish middle-aged man, a biker type, tattooed and all in black — black T-shirt, tight black Levi's, black boots, like the clothes they give you the day you get out of Folsom. Everyone knows you have to wear shorts up here in the heat, or your gauziest pants, billowing and worn-out such as the ones I was wearing, like Dustin Hoffman's in *Papillon*. The man looked angry. My arms bristled with goose bumps. Luckily, Lily appeared and ran up to investigate. She licked and nosed the man's hand. He reached into his pocket, and appeared to slip her something, a biscuit, perhaps, laced with strychnine. I tried to say something when we passed, but the words lodged in my throat: I squeaked hello, like a cartoon character: "Hi, Mr. Serial Killer — ow, ow!" He passed without speaking, hassled and frozen, like a snow globe of all the terror of the world.

All I had to protect me, besides Lily, was my ubiquitous pen, which, while mightier than the sword, was probably not going to do it if he lunged at me.

But strangely enough, he didn't. I continued walking.

Around another turn in the fire road, turkey vultures flopped around in the dirt, like the child. I'd often seen them overhead, lazy V's hanging in the sky, hissing, but I'd never seen them on the road. They are ugly birds, brown with wattley red heads, sort of testicular; but their genus name means "purifier," because they eat carrion and purify the countryside. It's a shame they don't eat dog doo, or spoiled toddlers. I wondered whether there were dead bodies nearby, bodies that the man in black had tossed down the hillside. Lily chased the vultures, her kilt flapping, and they took off, hissing as they flew away.

I tried to imagine what they'd been eating, and what they were saying to one another: "We can come back in an hour! We'll be hungry again by then."

Recycling is always going on up here, birth, death, compost. Alone in the hills, I can sometimes feel the people who have died, who stay near. I don't have a clue how the system works, but this is my belief. I can say "Hi, Pammy" or "Hi, Dad," and I can hear them say hi. I play their favorite music at home sometimes so we can hear it again together. I crank up *Kind of Blue* for them, by Miles Davis, who said, "Don't play what's there. Play what's not there." I feel them inside me and on my couch, listening with their eyes closed. Dad and Pammy both loved Mozart and jazz and folk music. I imagine life as a continuum, all sorts of comings and goings, as with the beings who climbed up and down Jacob's ladder, in the junction between heaven and earth, between the quick and the dead and the not yet born, the invisible beings here to help, moving to and fro, coming to help others move to and fro.

For me, personally, the system would be much clearer if God or life had installed a bald patch of grass between us, and wherever else there is. If anyone had thought to ask me.

The last people I ran into that day were a young man a little older than Sam and an older guy who had something nonspecifically wrong with him, an expression of not being all there. He moved with a halting, sluggish gait, and had a small beet-red head, like the vultures. The lenses in his horn-rimmed glasses were so thick that I wondered whether he was nearly blind. The young man looked a lot like Sam, and somehow managed to glide as he walked, like a warrior through tall grass.

We exchanged hellos. I have a funny habit I picked up from my father, who was also an avid hiker. Whenever he passed strangers on the path, he'd say hello in a friendly way, then dip his head and inhale with a sniffling sound, as if the air were freezing. He was secretly shy.

I made the puffy inhalation after I passed the men. At first I tried to invent a touching story for the young man walking with the older one — the heroic teenager with the simple and unsullied older man, from out of Rousseau. Then I figured we probably shared the same basic human condition: we went to plays we couldn't quite follow, we worried when we had to pee and there was no bathroom around, we fell into moods, both hopelessness and random silliness. The specifics might be different, but not the essence. We're not so special. That's the good and bad news.

Lily and I came to the poop baggies I'd left behind. I swept down on them where the grass met the road, as if they were Easter eggs. Lily, on the other hand, staggered with heat prostration. I wonder whether the beings on Jacob's ladder use an escalator now, whether they carry laptops or cell phones. I looked back at the ancient expanse of hills. You can almost imagine dinosaurs up here, or leopards. It's pure magic, like heaven or an Italian movie. How had it taken me nearly an hour to notice? Saint Paul, who can be such a grumpy book-thumper, said that where sin abounds, grace abounds, and I think this is Paul at his most insightful, hopeful, faithful, when it comes to politicians and to me — if by "sin" we mean strictly the original archery term of missing the mark. I realized just then that sin and grace are not opposites, but partners, like the genes in DNA, or the stages of child-birth. Labor was so much more painful than I could have ever imagined. I felt I might lose my mind. Sam's fist tore a small hole in my body, and it got infected. I had a high fever and chills. The nurses covered me with sheets they had warmed up that smelled like Ivory soap and antiseptic, and those mixed with the smells from my body, and my fear, and with the smells of my brother and best friend at my feet, saying, "Push. Push."

I remembered the sips of ice-cold apple juice the doctor gave me whenever I felt like giving up, like the occasional glimmers on these hillsides of what the landscape will look like when the rain starts to fall.

KOOKABURRA

The twentieth anniversary of my getting sober was last week, the day before my favorite annual church event, Faith Fair. This is a party the church throws for the children of the community, part of our Ministry of Joy. And twenty years is a landmark birthday. I've always believed that there was a certain age after which I would be all well and I'd stop feeling as if I'd been abandoned here on earth with no explanation. When I was little, the magic number was 6 — the first-graders had maturity, secret information (like gnostics), and lunch boxes. Then 13, 18, 21, and now, twenty years sober.

So the last thing I expected was to make a childish scene the weekend of the two events. All I can say is, Thank *God* there are no live feeds of our minds streaming online.

I've been in charge of Faith Fair for six years, an afternoon in early summer when we rent a colossal inflatable jump house, decorate our church courtyard with balloons and streamers and used-car-lot flags, and offer the families of the town lunch, sno-cones, face-painting, crafts. We help them make necklaces and wall hangings from clay. Everything is free, including the raffle tickets, which kids can use to win Frisbees stacked with cool little toys, or videos, or soccer balls. Our choir sings a set of our happier hymns — "Somebody Prayed for Me," "Leaning on the Everlasting Arms." You don't hear songs about Calvary. You don't hear "Go Down, Moses." Afterward we play loud classic gospel CDs, Aretha, Mahalia, Sam Cooke.

It takes a few of us working for weeks to pull it off. I get the equipment, some toys and art supplies; other people handle food, raffle items, music, decorations. We turn our fellowship hall into a crafts shop, so I buy beads, cord, and packs of the best clay, the softest to work with and the best to bake, in glorious colors. Every year I charge the two big-ticket items, the jump house and the balloon bouquets, and write checks for rubber balls, jump ropes, and bottles of bubbles.

The other volunteers and I gather at ten to set up, and then the jump-house guy ar-

rives and inflates the house on our lawn —
we always request the Blue Dog. Some of
us walk through the community, handing
out leaflets. At twelve we put out the first
platter of hot dogs. Parents from the other
five churches in town often arrive first, with
their kids in tow, or vice versa. This is a
troubled community, with a lot of darkness
and addiction alongside its riches, and
people from each church show up to help at
functions of the other churches — summer
recreation programs, tutoring during the
school year, mentoring, Vacation Bible
School, and things like our Faith Fair.

This year we had the usual beautiful
weather, the fabulous sticky children running around painted like princesses and
jaguars, practicing numa-numa dance steps
on the lawn (the first year of the fair it was
the Macarena), and jumping themselves
silly. I've taught some of them at Sunday
school since they were very young. I have
seen their first squiggles, on the light green
offering envelopes.

If people are attending the fair for the first
time, we show them our Sunday-school
classrooms. We have a sweet, simple pro-
gram: we focus on how much Jesus loves
them, on social justice, and on joy. We teach
them variations on Blake's great line that

we are here "to learn to endure the beams of love." We teach them to watch for beauty and to help however they can during catastrophes. We tell them to feed the poor and to feed one another. When you take food in that has been prepared with love, you take in other people. The children know this — I think they know much of what we do, way deep down. They know that they're made of the same stuff as Jesus and yet capable of the full range of human behavior. That the world is made up of illusion and trickery, and that God is everywhere. And that one day, they'll be like us. In the meantime, they gobble down hot dogs and bounce.

Faith Fair is one version of the story I love most. Every year we all race around like mad, and then no one shows up when we first open, and I always think we will flop this time. Dozens of kids begin arriving then, and I worry that there will be too *many* this year, and there won't be enough food or sno-cone syrup. Something inevitably goes wrong, someone gets hurt on the jump house or a bike gets stolen and the cops are called, and everything falls into wreckage at our feet. Then somehow — this is what the story is all about — things sort themselves out, and we start all over.

This year as I watched the kids, I thought

of how often, as my son has grown and the world has changed, I have told them updated accounts of this story. The gist of the story is that faith and grace will not look as they do in Bible stories, will not involve angels, flames, or harps. Disaster usually happens for me when everything I have counted on has stopped working, including all of my best skills, intentions, and good ideas. I overreact or shut down, then torture myself about what a fraud I am, like Kookaburra's bitter aunt Esther, in the branches of the old gum tree, pretending to sing the laughing song of the others but privately stewing. Usually there is something I can't climb over, all the tools and stepladders have broken, and no one is around to give me a leg up. No one comes along to say, "I'll haul you up, little lady." Some pitiful thing appears or occurs, entirely inadequate to help shift this grim situation, and it can't possibly be enough, but then it is.

Nothing went wrong this year at Faith Fair. None of the children got hurt on the jump house, none of the old people fainted in the heat, the PA system worked fine, the choir turnout was big. The pastor, who usually gets to be chairperson of the sno-cone ministry, got to hang out in the shade, talking to everyone who came by, and the teenage face-painters adorned every child.

At three in the afternoon, we sent people home, and the jump-house guy came and deflated the Blue Dog. The grown-ups stayed to clean, trudging around with aching feet and Hefty bags.

Late that night I e-mailed my bill to people on the fair committee. In early sobriety I heard that if you have an idea after ten p.m., it is probably not a good idea — and this was before e-mail. Still, I am always under budget, so even though my mind was a birdhouse of exhaustion, stressed from overstimulation that day, I sent out my bill.

At around eleven, I heard from one woman on the committee that everything looked fine. Then, at eleven-fifteen, I heard from another woman, who said that a man on the committee was sorry, but there was a new accounting system. This year we needed receipts: Visa bill, canceled checks.

A small voice inside me said, "Let this go until tomorrow." But the arrogant, wounded part was astounded. It said, *"Excuuuuuse me?"* I was exhausted, and it may just be that "system" is not my favorite word, especially when a man is trying to get me to conform to his, even when he is a good man and a casual church friend. In any case, I stared at the second e-mail like someone needing the Heimlich maneuver. Then I sat around glowering.

This reaction makes no sense at all to me. First of all, I love my church family more than life, and most of me knew that things would sort themselves out. Maybe this old, familiar anxiety helps me feel safe: maybe if I were ever to feel deep financial security and self-esteem, finally get it all just right, God would take me out with an air strike. I don't get it.

Except — in my defense — I come to my money nuttiness honestly. My parents had terrible problems with money; they never had enough. My mother grew up cold and poor in Liverpool, and money for her was like grades in school, it was about how you were doing in the world's eyes. If you had a nice pile when the winds howled, you'd be safe. Rich friends and movie stars had a glaze of smoothness, shininess, and troubles must surely slide off them. Horrible things could not crawl under or over their beautiful white picket fences. And my father was raised by stingy, repressed Presbyterian missionaries, for whom money was even more treacherous than sex. Manage your money, and you might be able to manage your more heinous appetites. Root of all evil, the devil, the Four Horsemen, and so on.

Let it be said, though, the lack of money is no great shakes, either. My father gave my mother a meager monthly budget. This was shaming and crazy-making and scary, because she had three kids, and pets, and no matter how inventively she served up ground beef and zucchini throughout the month, she couldn't make ends meet. She often had to go into my father's study to ask for more because the kitty had gotten sick or one of us had lost a shoe. I'd be doing homework with him when she came in, a supplicant with a bad attitude. He'd look down his nose at her, over the tops of his reading glasses, and slowly, like Bartleby, reach for the big black leather-bound check ledger he kept in his top drawer.

This was how it was for all her friends. This was the system before the women's movement.

We were not stupid children. You do not side with the unhappy person with the rice bowl. You align with the person who has power and the leather-bound company checkbook. I inwardly recoiled from my mother's neediness and rage.

Then both my parents died without leaving anything, so we three kids had money problems, too, which is to say no money.

I have worked for twenty years on getting over some of my fear and shame about money, and where has it gotten me? A letter arrives from the IRS, and before I open it I'm instantly thinking identity theft, arrest, liens, perp walks. I don't get it: If God has all the power and I've bravely shined so many flashlights into these dark corners, why doesn't God let me get well?

I reread the second e-mail. And then I ratted the man out: I e-mailed everyone on the committee, and included a copy to our pastor, so she could see how unjustly I was being treated, how I was being hassled. I wrote, "*Clearly,* I do not have what it takes to be a Presbyterian," which meant to be an anal-retentive petty bureaucrat. And, I added, "I simply cannot spend one more *second* on this matter." Then I hit Send.

I felt powerful and righteous, for several minutes. Then I felt like hell. I was a snitch. Why had I sent that e-mail? It was clearly the kind of thing you wrote to get off your chest but not to send. Now the real me was being revealed in the high school showers of life. You do so much learning and therapy and living, gleaning as much insight as you can, and you think you've won all these carnival tickets that you can cash in now — but the crabby, hairy-nosed old carny won't let you cash in the red tickets you've amassed in other realms. The prizes on the money shelf require *orange* tickets. And as with money, you never seem to have quite enough.

I could not go back. I needed a cooling-off period. But something in me cried out: Annie! Stop! Church is where your recovery began, a year before you got sober. This is about how weird your parents were about money, how your father withheld money from your mother, and how desperately you loved him. The guy at church is an innocent bystander. This is not your stuff. It's your mom's and dad's. The man didn't know your parents. How can he even be involved?

Finally I thought of one true thing, which is that sometimes I act just as juvenile as I ever did, but as I get older, I do it for shorter periods of time. I find my way back to the path sooner, where there is always one last resort: get a glass of water and call a friend.

I got some water and called a friend who always stays up late.

She was sound asleep.

But after I woke her, she insisted I tell her what was going on. I spilled it all out. I told her about Faith Fair, my mom's budget, my dad looking down his nose. She listened to how horrible it was, to my rationalizations. She laughed gently at the bad parts, and said, "Oh, hon," like a sweet waitress in a crappy coffee shop.

She did not say much, but let me get my guck into the air, so it was no longer in the anaerobic rat chamber of my mind. And as I told her my bleak and embarrassing story, it felt like dirty clothes. I'd been trying to wash and dry it inside myself, in my embarrassed mind, which doesn't really make much sense, laundry-wise. When you hang things outside, they get air, warmth, light; and you see that even with the stains and frayed collar, the garment has kept you covered and warm for a long time.

Then my friend spoke. She said that when she'd gotten sober, she saw that even though you get the monkey off your back, the circus never really leaves town. "Make yourself a nice snack," she told me.

I made oatmeal with applesauce.

The best way to change the world is to change your mind, which often requires feeding yourself. It makes for biochemical peace. It's almost like a prayer: to be needy, to eat, to taste, to be filled, building up instead of tearing down. You find energy to do something you hadn't expected to do, maybe even one of the holiest things: to go outside and stand under the stars, or to go for a walk in the morning, or in such hard times, both. But first I wrote back to everyone on the committee, plus the pastor, and said, I am sorry; ignore my earlier e-mail. Please forgive me. I wrote, "I know you already do." This made me feel like crying, because I was so grateful, and because I wished I had been kinder to my mother. By the next morning, before I left for church, everyone had e-mailed me back. The man wrote: "We are here with only love for you, Annie." I went outside and sat on the front step with my coffee and looked at the wild orange blossoms of the ginger plants in my garden until it was time to go.

ACKNOWLEDGMENTS

Gertrude Stein said that "silent gratitude isn't very much to anyone," and I am loudly grateful in my heart to a number of people.

Jake Morrissey at Riverhead has been a perfect new editor for me for a while now. Thank you also to Susan Petersen Kennedy, Geoff Kloske, and Mih-Ho Cha; to my copy editor, Anna Jardine; and to Craig Burke and Heather Connor.

Thank you to everyone at the Wylie Agency — Andrew, Edward Orloff, Liping Wang, and especially my agent and darling friend, Sarah Chalfant. Love to Nick, too.

Thank you, Lori Leibovich, my fabulous editor and friend at Salon, where some of these pieces first ran, and to Joan Walsh and David Talbot, who gave me total freedom.

Thank you to the people who help me write and who make my work so much better on a daily basis by being close, brilliant, inspiring, and articulate friends, especially

Doug Foster and Neshama Franklin. Thank you *loudly,* Karen Carlson, Geneen Roth, Mark Childress, Karl Fleming, Robyn Posin, and Father Tom Weston. It would be hard for me to explain how central you are to my work and my life.

Last, the hugest, deepest thank you to the Reverend Ms. Veronica Goines and all the people of St. Andrew Presbyterian Church, Marin City, California. Services at eleven.

PERMISSIONS

ABOUT THE AUTHOR

The bestselling author of *Plan B, Traveling Mercies,* and *Operating Instructions,* **Anne Lamott** is a past recipient of a Guggenheim Fellowship. A former columnist for *Salon* magazine, she lives near San Francisco.